101 fear of flying questions answered

Top tips from aviation experts and effective techniques to overcome your fears.

Published by Flying Without Fear Publishing

PO BOX 289, Betchworth. Surrey. RH3 7WX

This edition published 2008.

Flying Without Fear was established in 1997 by Virgin Atlantic to help people to beat their fear of flying.

British Library Cataloguing-in-Publication Data.

A catalogue record for this book is available from the British Library.

ISBN 978-0-9558145-0-1

Book cover designed by

hubanddesign

Brand & Packaging Specialists

tel: 0116 255 0014
email: design@hubanddesign.co.uk
www.hubanddesign.co.uk

Aircraft Cartoon by Alan Evans
www.madetomeasuretraining.co.uk

Technically edited by Captain Dominic Riley, Airbus Fleet, Virgin Atlantic Airways and
Dr Jason Ian Broch MBChB BSc (hons).

Special contributions, David Landau for relaxation tips, David Gott for Cabin Crew Section,
Captain Jeremy Burrows for technical editing.

Production and design by Lorna Wootton

Proof read by: Judith Instone, Janine Skidmore, David Gott, Capt Burrows and Mrs Conway.

Press Reviews and Testimonials

"Virgin's Flying Without Fear day could be the best gift you ever gave anyone." *The Financial Times*

"It's perfectly curable. For a fail-safe solution, try a fear of flying course…The best is Flying Without Fear, run by Virgin Atlantic." *The Times, Travel Magazine*

"The pilots, David Kistruck and Dominic Riley, were brilliant. They were funny and kept the atmosphere relaxed yet informative." *Neil Moore, Metro newspaper*

"What an amazing course! I absolutely loved it. When I flew out of London the next day, on a genuine flight, I was so armed with knowledge about how a plane works, I felt like I could have piloted the big bird." *Eve Conant, Vogue*

The Eastern Daily Press reported "the infectious enthusiasm of the (Flying Without Fear) team is undoubtedly a factor in its success rate."

Sunday Express reporter, Louise Earl "I can't believe it. I loved it and to be up above the clouds was just brilliant. Orlando here I come."

Hello magazine ran a full page article on how the reigning Miss England, Eleanor Glynn, wouldn't travel to the Miss World competition in Poland due to her life long fear of flying, until she attended the Virgin Atlantic Flying Without Fear course. After the course she flew to Poland and was quoted saying " The flight to Warsaw was brilliant. I never thought I'd hear myself say I enjoyed a flight!"

The Sunday Times reporter Liz Edwards "…there are several spontaneous rounds of applause, and on landing, when the pilot asks if we want to go again, there's an enthusiastic response."

Airliner World, "Many of those on the course were actually quite surprised at how effective the days session had been. 'I attended a fear of flying course with another airline about 10 years ago but with no success, so I was way apprehensive. But there was no need to be, because I thoroughly enjoyed this course. The whole day was very relaxed and held in a very friendly atmosphere which made all the difference' said Christine Milland."

South Manchester Reporter's Kate Stirrup, "The Virgin staff were wonderful ... this was a life changing experience ...The difference this course – just one day – has made to the way I look at air travel really is remarkable ... if you are scared of flying, this course could be one of the best investments of your life."

Shropshire Star's Ben Bentley, "Upon touchdown there were tears of joy and hugs. We have survived the plane and all the fears attached to it, and this is no small victory."

Scotland on Sunday's Ruth Fairbain, "At the beginning of the day I was absolutely certain there was no way I was setting foot on a plane, that I would be content to come and listen and try to work on my fears from there. But when the moment came, I was more than happy. I felt really relaxed and confident."

A reporter for Newsshopper called Louise Tweddell, "I was genuinely not scared. As we took off I was amazed to feel none of the usual symptoms of fear ... As we landed there was a huge cheer, caused by a sense of achievement. I got off the plane feeling like I had beaten it."

Mark Stratton, Wanderlust magazine, "After circling cloudless skies, we returned to earth. Applause broke out on touchdown ... behind me I heard an excited voice comment: Shame there wasn't a little more turbulence."

In the Newcastle Evening Chronicle, Patricia Stobbs, "I now go to bed dreaming of where I'm going to fly."

Brighton Argus reporter Ruth Addicott, ".......And for the first time in years, I didn't feel scared but actually enjoyed the experience. After what seemed like no time, it was over and another big cheer went up when we touched down. For anyone afraid of flying, I'd definitely recommend it."

Southern Daily Echo, Paula Rushton "Imagine your worst fear. Now imagine deliberately putting yourself in the path of that fear. I did and it was fantastic!"

Surrey Advertiser Julia Hunt, "As the minutes ticked by the mood on board got better and better and by the time we landed everybody – including myself – was euphoric."

Now magazine Gemma McCafferty "That sick, panicky sensation is a thing of the past and I feel I can do anything. My phobia's well and truly gone."

Welcome from Sir Richard Branson

Congratulations!

You have just made a very wise buy here.

I have been very close to Richard and Paul who have brought this book to you, ever since we set up Virgin Atlantic's 'Flying Without Fear' course all those years ago.

The courses have been very popular and I hear of countless stories of people now starting to enjoy their lives fully.

I have been very fortunate to have enjoyed a lifetime of flying around the world – I don't want you to miss out on another flight ever again.

Enjoy the book and hope to see you flying Virgin Atlantic Airways!

Take care

Sir Richard Branson
President Virgin Atlantic Airways

Why this book?

We are here to help you to beat your fear. We have been running fear of flying courses every month since November 1997 and in that time have changed thousands of people's lives.

We know that the reason you are reading this now is that you have decided ENOUGH IS ENOUGH! You no longer want this fear and you are ready to do something different. Well, this book is literally jam - packed full of essential information and tips that you can read and use today.

This book is for you if:

- You do fly, but dread it for months before the flight.

- You have had a bad experience and you have said 'That's it!'

- You have never flown because you have been put off by what you have heard about it.

- You feel trapped in an aircraft and it is getting worse.

We have combined information and help in an easy to digest, light-hearted style that will give you help TODAY with your fear. We have pooled some of the questions that we get asked on our courses and our message board and they have been answered by experts in a light-hearted and honest way – in normal language.

It is sad, but true to say, that most of the people you talk to about your fear of flying don't really understand what it is like. They may tell you to just get over it! They are well meaning but just don't know what to do. Within minutes of reading this book, you will already be moving towards your well deserved goal of beating the fear and opening the world back up to you.

Contents

Hello from the team

Richard Conway BA (hons) Professional Training and Development – Co Founder

Welcome to our book from Virgin Atlantic's 'Flying Without Fear' team.

Our objectives are to share our passion, knowledge, insights and also the fun element that reflects how we run our courses, in order to help you to overcome your fear of flying.

In case you're now thinking, 'these people can't possibly know how I feel, as they've never had a fear of flying', I'd like to tell you my story.

When I was young, I flew to various parts of the world with my parents. I didn't love flying when I was younger, but I certainly wasn't fearful of it.

In 1993, when I was 21, I was unwell and I just happened to be travelling to Rome by air at the time with some work colleagues. That day, I couldn't even manage to put my hand in my pocket to buy duty free (for those who know me, that's a big deal!) and after that illness, I associated that time of illness with travelling onboard an aircraft, even though there was nothing wrong with the actual flight at all.

Looking back, now that I am totally fearless, I know that I had a fear of feeling as if I did at the time I was ill. It made me feel like I wasn't in control and anything could happen to me. Over time, I just continued to avoid flying at all and the more I avoided it, the more I became fearful of it. I kept making excuses and these fears always used to be reinforced by certain things, such as media stories.

In the late 1990's, I decided that I had to find help as I'd holidayed Cornwall and Centreparcs to death. I became so desperate to beat the fear, I just wanted to hire a commercial jet aircraft and a very knowledgeable senior pilot. I felt so bad I did not even care what it cost!

I then envisaged going up in that aircraft with the captain. I was hoping that I could then understand how everything worked and I knew I'd get a feeling of control back and therefore confidence, by gaining this knowledge.

I called around many of the UK's airports and no-one could help me. I was only offered suggestions such as going to visit a psychologist or hypnotist. I knew what I needed was knowledge from people that I trusted. I also called many airlines to find this help and charter a commercial jet and pilot. Unsurprisingly, no-one took me seriously, that is until I came across Virgin Atlantic.

Paul Tizzard at Virgin Atlantic did take me seriously and Paul, who'd already set up very small group talks on 'fear of flying' in 1997, put me in touch with one of the senior captains for help. This captain, Norman Lees, helped me to overcome my fear. Being a businessman with a background in Business and Professional Training and Development, I thought if I needed this and couldn't find relevant help, so must some other people and I then went on a mission to help! I set up the One-on-One 'Flying Without Fear' course for Virgin Atlantic. There was nothing like this at all on offer in the industry and we had lots of people sign up.

Paul, who also had a training and psychology background, and I, together went on to start the Virgin Atlantic group

'Flying Without Fear' courses, which we passionately believe in. The courses have proved very popular and I believe that this is due to our exceptional team. The Eastern Daily Press put it well by saying 'the infectious enthusiasm of the (Flying Without Fear) team is undoubtedly a factor in its success rate.' We have helped many thousands of people to date. We have a message board on our **www.flyingwithoutfear.info** website that shows feedback, from some of those who've attended our courses, posted directly from their own e-mail addresses. Please do take a look. It's an interesting read and shows it from their individual perspectives.

Enjoy the read!

Richard Conway

Director, Virgin Atlantic's 'Flying Without Fear' programme.

Paul Tizzard BSc. (hons) Psychology- Co Founder

This book is about giving you the information that you need to beat your fear!

I have been personally involved with this programme since its inception in David Landau's (our psychotherapist) hallway where it was first conceived in March 1997. A short letter to Richard Branson later and within 12 months it was up and running.

We know that the people who attend our courses are often very successful in other areas of their life. We have always approached these courses from the point of view that people are intelligent but are just being held back by this terrible fear.

Well, help is here!

I passionately believe that anything is possible once you have made the decision to commit to that thing.

We wrote this book, because we know people can beat this fear and they do. Most people who come on our courses tell us that they are now totally cured. For other people, it goes a long way to getting their lives back in order. I know that you have fears that are individual to you and I know that this book will give you the chance to get some of your questions answered.

I hope that you find this useful and I wish you every success with beating your fear.

Best wishes

Paul Tizzard

Director, Virgin Atlantic's 'Flying Without Fear' Programme.

David Gott

I have been involved with Virgin Atlantic's 'Flying Without Fear' Course since 2003. I personally speak at most of the courses about why Cabin Crew are actually on board the aircraft and the training that they go through. In this book, I have helped with the technical editing plus, there are some notes from my talk towards the rear of this book.

I joined Virgin Atlantic in 1989 and have enjoyed every minute of seeing all those fantastic places. I work now as a senior safety training instructor in the Cabin Safety Training Department.

The main reason cabin crew are carried on board is for safety and security of the aircraft, passengers and crew. Thankfully many people will only ever see the customer service side of things i.e. the serving of drinks, meals and duty-free. However should a situation arise, the cabin crew are trained to deal with any eventuality that could happen on board an aircraft.

Cabin crew training in all airlines is made up of three elements, Service Training, Aviation Medicine Training and Cabin Safety Training. It is the service on board and Cabin environment that makes the airlines different, but all the other elements are made up of legal requirements. There are requirements crew must learn and pass before they get their prized "wings".

Cabin Crew are trained in much more than just first aid which is why it is now called Aviation Medicine. The aircraft cabin is a unique environment which is why they have specialist training. There is also medical equipment that crew are trained to use on board. Cabin Crew can deal with a minor headache right up to childbirth.

Safety and security are at the heart of commercial aviation. Much of the training takes place practically in cabin mock ups that make things as realistic a possible. These practical elements are assessed as well as taking written exams which must also be passed.

Enjoy the book and maybe I will meet you on one of our courses.

Best wishes

David Gott

Captain Dominic Riley

I am a captain with Virgin Atlantic, currently flying the Airbus A340 all over the world.

I started flying with the RAF in 1977 and after 3 years of flying training I was sent to Germany to fly the Phantom F4 as a fighter pilot specialising in low-level air defence. Another F4 tour followed at RAF Leuchars in Scotland and then an instructional tour on the Hawk aircraft. In 1987 a dream came true when I was selected onto the RAF display team the Red Arrows for a 3 year tour of duty. After the best 3 years of my life reality returned with a posting back to the frontline once again flying the F4 Phantom. Then in 1996 I decided that the RAF would have to cope without me as I wished to become a commercial pilot.

I was very fortunate that Virgin Atlantic were recruiting at the time and I became an Airbus A340 first officer with Virgin. In 2001 I was selected for command training and was promoted to captain to fly the Airbus A320 with Virgin throughout Europe. Then in 2002 I returned to the long-haul life back on the A340 where I am currently employed.

I joined the Virgin Atlantic 'Flying Without Fear' team in 2000 and have been actively involved with it since then. I have helped thousands of nervous flyers just like you. I am passionate about helping people to overcome their fear of flying and I know that if you read this book you will benefit not just from my many years of flying experience but also from all the other contributors varied experiences. All of us are part of the great Virgin Atlantic 'Flying Without Fear' team and I wish you every success.

As an Ex-Red arrow pilot I know a thing or two about teamwork and this book has been put together by our fabulous 'Flying Without Fear' team. Helping you to overcome your fear of flying is our aim – I hope that you enjoy the contributions from us all.

I look forward to meeting you on one of our courses.

Best wishes

Captain Dom Riley

David Landau – Consultant Psychoanalyst

David has been in practice at his clinic in London for many years as a psychoanalyst. He has developed a form of therapy called "Interactive Mind Communication".

This combines deep relaxation with positive suggestions and this simple process helps people to overcome fears and phobias. He shows people how to take control of their minds instead of allowing their minds to control them; how to start doing things that they have not been able to start and how to stop doing things that they have been unable to stop!

In a sentence, he helps people to start really living instead of just "existing"! David has appeared on national television, Capital and BBC Radio and regularly gives talks all over the UK and US.

Dr Jason I Broch MBChB, BSc. (Hons)

I qualified in medicine in 1997 and now work as a GP in Leeds where I am a partner. As a GP it is always important to keep improving my skills and knowledge so I have taken time out from my training to undertake some research and gained my BSc.

As well as General Practice, I have been involved with several companies, helping to bring healthcare products to market. In particular, some of these products have brought me to be heavily involved with the aviation industry, hence I am the medical editor of this book.

I hope that you enjoy reading this book and find it useful.

Very best wishes

Jason Broch

101 of the most frequently asked fear of flying questions

Answered for you.

The questions below have come from two sources. Some are straight from the message board on our **www.flyingwithoutfear.info** website, where people can post questions at any time they like. These have been reproduced faithfully with their answers.

The second group have been compiled from our course over the last ten years. They have been reproduced exactly as some of our clients wrote them. Some of the questions and postings are quite frank and that is why we have left them exactly as they are so that the richness is not lost.

1   *I feel out of control when I am on the aircraft - what can I do about it?*

Let's talk about control or lack of control. This is an interesting one for us. We know that the people that come on our courses are intelligent and capable people. In many other aspects of their lives they are extremely successful. For some reason, this fear is the one that eludes them. The one that they cannot shake off! Why is that? As you will see below, there are millions of reasons for it and your reason will be personal to you!

Lack of control could be defined as, 'When the presenting circumstances are perceived to be beyond what the individual thinks he/she can deal with.' In other words, something happens and we tell ourselves that it is more than we can cope with. At some point in our brain, a switch goes on that says, 'whoaaaa - this is too much for me!'

The reality is that we are not in control in most aspects of our lives. We will say to ourselves, 'I am in control when I am driving my car.' 'I can pull over, speed up, stop and get out.' Yes, of course we can do that. However, was your car's engine oils (all of them) checked within the last 24 hours? Do you have several backup systems, as an aircraft does, for each component within your car should they fail? Do you re-sit your driving test every 6 months? The pilots of commercial aircraft have to be tested that often in a simulator on a pass or fail basis. Every year, they also sit an instrument flying test and in addition, an operational proficiency test in front of a senior training captain.

This is meant to be facetious as we don't really have 'control' over our vehicles, the road conditions and especially not the other drivers. It is likely that we will pass our driving test at about 17 or 18 years of age and not be expected to do one again until we are about 70!

The point we are making here is that it is true; you are not in control of the aircraft. (A point I am personally very happy about!) The people that are in control of the aircraft are not occasional pilots. They are professionals who are tested every six months on their abilities to fly. They are tested medically every year. They are conscious that they can lose their licence at any time if they do not pass the stringent tests.

So, in summary, we are not in control. The pilots are. But I challenge you to find a more professional group of people to look after you. Remember, they are also on the same aircraft. They also have families that they want to get back to. Commercial aviation is a business where safety comes before business. Safety is always the first priority.

2   *I have claustrophobia - what can be done?*

We use a mixture of three things on our courses and the same applies to our book: Honesty, Humour and Knowledge.

Let's use some honesty … Aircraft can feel like enclosed spaces to people. More honesty … When you get on board, the door is shut and you cannot get out … You cannot open the door. This is a good thing.

The moment that the door shuts, your mind can go into panic overdrive. Your brain is attempting to protect you from what you see as a threat and you can feel that you have to escape. Maybe similar feelings to what you may have if you were in a lions den, with the lion in there too! To those who suffer with this, it can be the most awful thing. You may experience sweaty palms, over breathing, anxiety and even 'tunnel vision.'

Two ways to control this aspect of your fear is to manage your breathing and your thoughts.

Breathing.

On our course, we spend a fair amount of time practicing breathing techniques to keep your breathing in control. Everything is linked to your breathing, if you don't control your breathing, everything else goes crazy such as your heart, your lungs, your thoughts etc.

Thoughts.

'It is not what happens to you but your interpretation of what happens to you.' Steven Covey. This is the basis of this cognitive approach. You need to become aware of what the 'chatterbox' in your head is saying.

Compare the two following thought patterns:

Chatterbox out of control.	Chatterbox in control.
'Oh my God, what was that noise?! It must mean we are crashing. I am not ready to die. The entire cabin crew look scared, it must be true.'	'Oh my God, what was that noise?! Okay, I may not feel comfortable but I am safe. If there was something I needed to know, the captain would have told me. Flying is safe. I am able to cope with whatever happens to me.'

Which of the above is going to leave you feeling more resourceful?

So to summarize, Fear of enclosed spaces is natural. It is an enclosed space. We suggest controlling two things to help you with this; your breathing and your thoughts.

3   *What is turbulence?*

Questions about Turbulence come up on each and every course that we have run since November 1997. It is one of the biggies for people.

This content is cribbed from listening to our pilots describing in terms that we all can understand. It is divided into two parts.

19

The first part looks at the reality of what turbulence does to an aircraft and you. The second part looks at what turbulence is in normal speak.

By the way, if you ever watch a programme on the TV which shows turbulence, it probably looks slightly dramatic! Some TV I have seen has made me think that if turbulence was like that, even I wouldn't get on an aircraft - Ever!

Unfortunately, TV films portray it with flashing lights and lots of weird engine noises. If you watch anything like this, please remember it is television not real life! Read on here and you will know that for certain!

We shall deliberately keep this all as straightforward as possible. Air has many of the properties of a fluid except the most obvious one, you can't see it. But that doesn't mean it's not there! The air that the aircraft is flying through is always moving around, just as the sea does and just as a river does. And in much the same way as the sea or the river moves, or 'wobbles' then so does the air. Obviously, any boat on the sea will pitch and roll in accordance with the movement of the water and in the same way the aircraft pitches and rolls as it is affected by the moving air. It is this phenomenon that we call turbulence.

One thing to state loud and clear from the start is this: Turbulence is not dangerous.

The reason that the captain turns on the seat belt sign either just prior to or just after encountering turbulence is to ensure that none of the passengers stumbles and falls over. It is also to prevent passengers from trying to get their heavy hand luggage out of the overhead lockers and possibly dropping it on an unsuspecting and possibly snoozing fellow traveller! Sometimes the captain asks the cabin crew to take their seats, this does not mean that the turbulence is becoming more dangerous (remember, turbulence is not dangerous in the first place!) but is simply a precaution to prevent the cabin crew from stumbling into the very heavy and hard edged catering trolleys.

Turbulence is very difficult to forecast accurately. But rest assured, if we know turbulence is likely to occur on your flight the captain will make an announcement to let you know that everything is well. This should help you to relax.

Remember: Turbulence is not dangerous.

4   *I have a fear of crashing.*

We want to help stop that happening to you. Stop the fear being in control of you instead of the other way around. I bet that you would like that too?

We run an activity at the beginning of every course to find out what people want from the day and this comes up every time.

The answer that follows may surprise you but we will explain.

You have every right to be scared of crashing. I am scared of crashing. Fear of dying is a rational fear. Who wants to die? No-one does.

What we forget when we think about all of the horrific things that could happen to us in an aircraft, is that we are guilty of allowing our thinking to become faulty.

How dare you say that?!

Well, it is true because if you want to be more at risk, travel by coach, travel by car, walk behind donkeys, ride a motorbike, ride a push bike or take any other form of transport than aircraft. Flying in commercial aircraft with all their law enforced safety checks is safer than any other form of transport.

Fact. The most dangerous part of a commercial pilot's day is his/her journey on the motorway to the airport.

The airline industry is an industry where safety always comes first before profit. Without safety there are no customers.

Commercial aircraft are safer than any other form of transport – even walking. The training and regulations in place for all pilots, cabin crew, engineers and air traffic controller is quite staggering. More than you hear about because it does not make the news.

'Today, one million people landed safely at their destination and nothing happened.' This is a headline that does not sell newspapers (although the Virgin Atlantic 'Flying Without Fear' team have all agreed that we would buy one!)

If an aircraft wing-tip brushes against a catering van at Heathrow airport, causing no damage to the aircraft and no danger to the passengers, it would probably be in the newspaper as, 'Aircraft Collides with Catering Van at Heathrow.'

So, coming back to crashing. It is normal to fear crashing as it is normal to fear dying – lots of people do. We have to do something about the way we think about this. Only we can control the thoughts in our head otherwise they control us.

Forgive us as we suggest that we have a choice here. If we want to think about dying we have two options open to us:

Option 1

Build 'thinking about dying' into everything we now do where it could happen such as eating peanuts, drinking beer, opening the door to a stranger, changing a plug socket and driving to work.

Option 2

Accept that dying and crashing are things that are normal to fear, HOWEVER, it is not normal to pinpoint all of that fear into one mode of transport. Especially, as the one that we are picking on is the one we are least likely in which to die.

Hopefully, you can see the irony in this? These comments are not intended to poke fun at the way our brains work sometimes. It is about thinking about it rationally.

We have to train ourselves to stop thinking about the worst possible consequences and learn to replace these with rational thoughts.

Top Tips:

Each and every time you think about catastrophe shout 'STOP' in your head (out loud if you prefer but not at work!)

Say instead something like, 'It is okay to feel worried as I am in the safest place I could be ... in an aircraft.' Or just simply, 'Everything is okay.'

We know it may sound twee - but it works. It takes effort because we have probably had years of telling ourselves 'I might die on this flight!'

Imagine the situation in your brain, you currently have a neural pathway the size of a motorway that links all things aircraft-related to feeling fearful. We get really good at bringing on the fear and do it even quicker the more we practice.

We are asking you to practice stopping the negative self talk and replace it with more positive talk. It is the equivalent of driving down a new dirt track to get somewhere versus going on the motorway. Slow but over time dirt tracks can become busy roads.

In summary - we have pointed out it is normal to fear crashing. The main point is that we need to re-train ourselves to put the fear of dying on an aircraft into perspective. We all will die in due course, but it is exceptionally unlikely to be in an aircraft.

5   *I hate all the weird noises that aircraft make.*

There are all sorts of noises on aircraft. You have told us that the bings and bongs can be frightening. Many people think that they're secret messages from the pilots to the cabin crew, which they're not. It can simply be a member of cabin crew letting their colleagues know that they'd like to communicate with them, so they may be asking them to pick up the phone. It maybe that they'd like to ask something as simple as 'have you got any more vegetarian meals available at your end of the aircraft?' It makes much more sense to communicate by phone, than to run down the length of the aircraft to find out.

Engines also make unfamiliar noises during the different stages of the flight. One of the most frightening noises according to what you tell us, is the engines at start-up. First, one engine will start and then another etc. It may also change the sound of the air conditioning on the aircraft temporarily. These noises are all absolutely normal.

When the undercarriage is raised after take off, or lowered before landing, there will be a vibration and mild clunking noise. This is completely normal.

If you don't know what you are listening to, it can seem pretty daunting.

We are here right now to tell you that all the noises you hear are normal, even those funny creaking noises that the overhead lockers make during take off and landing. All is normal - they are meant to do that. They have been designed to flex and rattle a little.

You can do one of a couple of things if you fear the noises onboard an aircraft:

1. Ask a member of the crew what the noise is, if you are concerned about a noise you hear

2. Re-train your brain to say that the noises are normal. What you are hearing is over emphasized because you are in an alien environment. An environment where everything just happens without you doing anything or anyone consulting you!

In summary. The noises on aircraft can appear quite weird. Just because you don't recognize them, does not make them dangerous. If in doubt, ask a member of the crew.

6   *What happens if all the engines fail and we fall out of the sky?*

Now we are talking about a major subject for a lot of people, which is Engine Failure.

There is a lot of misunderstanding around engines. These engines are not like your car engine. They cost a vast sum of money to make and buy and are incredibly reliable.

There is a huge amount of money spent on maintaining them too.

But, let's take the worst scenario possible.

You are flying along and the aircraft's engines fail.

What do you think would happen?

A The Aircraft would plummet immediately into the ground, or;

B The Aircraft would glide until the pilots landed it or whilst he or she restarts the failed engine(s).

The answer is B.

The airplane is a huge glider. This is the same regardless of how heavy the aircraft is. The engines are needed to power the aircraft for take off and climb and keep the aircraft at height. However, it is the wings that provide the lift for flight. And no, the wings cannot fall off. Think about glider pilots flying gliders, these have no engines at all but are completely safe to fly.

The aircraft will glide if the engines stop working.

Here are a few key points.

1 When the pilots plan the take off, they allow in their calculations for the possibility of an engine failure at the most critical time. By the way, this is extremely rare due to the modern Jet engines being so incredibly reliable.

2 The pilots practice the scenario of engine failure several times per year in their simulators and they have to practice flying without the full complement of engines and landing safely.

3 The pilots know at all times on a flight, exactly where the closest airfield is and would use this as a diversion if necessary.

The world of aviation is not like other transport industries. Airlines can't afford for things to go wrong. Modern Jet Engines are so incredibly reliable now and safety ALWAYS comes first.

So, if you did ever have an engine failure on one of your flights, which is highly unlikely, it is not a problem for the pilots.

Aircraft can fly at speed on one engine safely if needs be and do remember that they can glide with no engines.

You may wonder 'Oh, *but what about two engine aircraft then?*'

Two engine aircraft have enough power in the other engine to take off if necessary. They have to because Airlines put safety first. Without safety there is no business.

Summary. Engine failure is extremely rare. Pilots plan take offs with the safety margin of one engine not working into the calculations. Even with no engines, the aircraft can glide. So relax, leave all these concerns behind you and enjoy the flight safe in the knowledge that the pilots are extremely well trained, tested regularly and just like you, want to complete the flight safely.

7 *With all this terrorist activity, flying can hardly be safe now can it?*

This is a very current one after the events of September 11th 2001. It is fair to say that the world has changed since then.

Every industry and the people within it, worldwide since then, approach security completely differently.

The horrific events of September 11th have had a major impact on the whole aviation industry and in fact the whole of the world.

The procedures now in place since that event have changed dramatically.

Terrorists tend to go for soft targets.

They go for areas that will cause the maximum disruption to others without themselves getting caught.

Airlines are not soft targets. There is so much more that has been added to the procedures at airports. There are things that you can see such as the longer times to check in now due to your bags being screened with more scrutiny.

There are lots of things that go on security-wise that you won't see and as non-airline security people, we may never know about.

Things that have been added at the airport security include:

- All bags are screened several times.

- From the moment that you book, passenger profiling takes place.

- Some Airlines have sky marshals on some flights.

- A bullet proof and attack proof door blocks the Flight Crew off. There is a door entry system that the cabin crew use to check on the pilots regularly. The flight deck door has a camera fitted near by which allows the pilots to see who is trying to gain access to the flight deck. The pilots can then prevent the door being opened if necessary.

The events of Sept 11th were horrific and shocked the world, but changed the nature of airline security forever.

The whole travel industry has had to improve security and they have done so. Airlines are not a soft target.

Summary. Terrorism has increased the perceived risk of travel for most of us. Things have changed in the airports dramatically since the September 11th attacks. There is a lot that goes on now to keep flying safe and most of it we won't know about as passengers.

8 What stops aircraft just falling out of the sky?

Here are some reasons why you might think and some answers to hopefully help you ...

When aircraft are up at height and traveling along at 400 miles an hour in clear open space, what is there to suddenly make it fall out of the sky?

Imagine driving along the motorway at 70 miles an hour and you suddenly turned the engine off, what would happen?

Your car would slow down gradually until it came to a gentle stop. If you happened to be at the top of a massive hill it might never slow down and could even speed up a bit depending on how steep the hill was. This is the effect of gravity.

Now imagine your worst scenario and at 30,000 feet up in the air, all of the aircraft engines suddenly stopped working.

The engines all stop. What happens to the aircraft? It glides remember and as the aircraft is gliding, you will be using gravity too to pick up speed because you will increase the air flow across the wings.

But how far would you glide for then?

Well if you were 30,000 feet up in the air, you would glide quite comfortably approximately three miles for every 1,000 feet of altitude. So, you would glide for approx 90 miles and you could land without engines too.

In Summary.

Aircraft do not just fall out of the sky. They have huge momentum as they are travelling at speeds of anything up to 500 miles per hour.

9   With all the cheap tickets nowadays, isn't it a matter of time before we run out of fuel and plummet to the ground?

Not possible because airlines always carry much more fuel than they need. Before take off, the pilots decide on at least two alternative airfields close to the destination at which they would land if the destination was not accepting aircraft for some reason. Enough fuel is carried to complete the planned flight, divert if necessary and then hold overhead the diversion airfield for over half an hour before finally landing. When all of this fuel is calculated a further 5% or so is added as a further safety margin.

10   How many people would be killed if lightning struck the aircraft?

None. Lightning has no effect on the aircraft as it is not earthed. There are static conducting rods attached to the rear of the aircraft that discharge the electricity. The wiring looms are made such that they are protected too. Sometimes when an aircraft is struck by lightning, it may leave tiny pin pricks to the outer shell of the aircraft. This is only the outer shell and does no harm to the people inside it. Lightning seems a little dramatic if it was nearby but absolutely nothing would happen to the aircraft.

11 *I am worried that a huge bird strike might bring the aircraft down?*

The engines are spread well apart far wider than the average flock of birds. Engines are tested at manufacture by firing dead poultry at them to make sure that they keep going. Also, many airports keep birds of prey to stop other birds thinking it is a good idea to hang around there. Airport staff drive around in vans playing bird of prey noises to scare them off. ALSO aircraft take off and land with full lights on as it has been shown to disturb the birds. There are no known birds which form flocks large enough to span the whole width of something like a 747. It might concern you, but as Capt Dominic Riley would say: 1lb pigeon versus 400 ton commercial jet – who's going to win!?

12 *I heard that Volcano dust once stopped all four engines on a 747?*

This did happen many years ago before anyone had thought of this event happening. However after the aircraft had glided through the volcanic dust cloud, engines restarted and the aircraft landed safely. Nowadays, each and every commercial flight has the location of volcanoes positioned on the flight routing and if there is any likelihood of the volcano being active, then the aircraft route takes it upwind of the location. This virtually guarantees the possibility of an all engine flame out never occurring again.

13 What would happen if a Pilot dies?

There are always a minimum of two pilots both capable of flying to the same standard. On the longer routes, there are sometimes up to four pilots. Cabin crew are trained in how to remove the pilot from his or her seat should they need to.

14 What would happen if the autopilot failed?

The autopilot is there to assist the pilot. All aircraft can be flown manually and every pilot is practiced in this skill. There are also back up auto pilot systems in case this happens.

15 How quickly would we die if the masks came down?

There are two types of decompression that would trigger the masks coming down. A slow decompression happens slowly over time. The aircraft cabin pressure is artificially set at around 7,000 feet. If the systems detected this pressure falling, the masks would come down. A slow leak of pressure could cause this to happen slowly. A hole blown in the side of the aircraft would create a rapid decompression, but this is extremely unlikely.

Masks would come down as soon as the pressure got to 14,000 feet. The Oxygen systems contain enough to keep us alive. The pilots would then descend the aircraft to 10,000 ft. where we can breathe normally anyway. There would be enough oxygen in the masks to manage this manoeuvre before we got to the level where we can breathe normally anyway. The pilots have their own oxygen system.

16 *I work in I.T. and our computers fail all the time. Why won't they do that up there?*

There are always back up computers for all major systems. They are manufactured in completely different companies and run on different software so that there is no risk of software contamination. Plus, no aircraft is entirely dependant on computers, they are simply there to make the flight more efficient.

17 *What happens when the hydraulics fail?*

There are always spare systems that can take over. Often up to three back up systems that can be used. On a lot of the aircraft hydraulic systems, there are ways to operate manually too.

18 *I suffer from panic attacks – what can be done for me?*

In our experience, Panic Attacks occur very rarely on our course itself. In fact, in ten years of running this course, we have only experienced two people having panic attacks, both of whom we were able to help to calm down naturally.

If you do, which is very unlikely by the time you are with us, you could not be in better hands. Cabin crew are trained to help you on regular flights.

It is often the fear of panic attacks for a lot of people which never manifests in reality.

For those of you that have had full blown panic attacks, you will know what a terrifying experience it can be for you and for those around you.

Why is it so terrifying?

Well, let's consider the following two sets of symptoms:

Panic Attack.	Heart Attack
Overheating	Overheating
Sweating	Sweating
Clammy hands	Clammy hands
Tunnel vision	Tunnel vision
Pains in chest	Pains in chest
Extreme anxiety and feeling of losing control	Extreme anxiety and feeling of losing control
Rapid breathing	Rapid breathing
Feel like you are going to die.	Feel like you are going to die.

Now, one of the above you could die from and one you won't. A Panic Attack won't kill you.

It feels like you are going to die and it is no laughing matter.

Panic attacks are the body's natural response to a situation that it feels are beyond what it can cope with.

Did you say natural?

Yes, it is natural and is very closely linked to the Fight or Flight instinct that all animals have.

In a panic attack, people will either panic and run away or panic and freeze.

So, what can be done?

We are now coming back to what we talked about earlier.

You can control your thoughts and your breathing.

We can teach you how to control your fear but YOU need to practice it to make it work.

Please give yourself every chance of success by starting the positive thinking practice now, today. Please don't wait till you are marching through the airport before you start chanting, I MUST RELAX, I MUST RELAX!

This is not meant to patronise but there are no magic cures.

It is very easy to get into faulty ways of operating; Faulty ways of thinking.

A personal story.

Paul is absolutely terrified of Big Wheels at fairgrounds. He hates them. The mere sight of one fills him with fear and dread. He knows that as soon as his kids see it, they will want to go on it. I don't imagine that he will ever love the big wheel.

Paul says, I use these techniques plus others from our course to control my fear.

I went on a big wheel two days ago. Two days before, I told myself I would be on it come what may. There was no way I was going to pass my fear onto my daughters ...

I noticed that within myself it was very easy to slip into faulty thinking. I saw myself strewn at the bottom of the big wheel in a lump of folded flesh. I could see it in vivid detail.

At that moment, I shouted STOP to myself.

Instead, I change my self talk to something positive to replace the negative talk.

We know that before an emotional response such as panic, there is a series of unhelpful thoughts. If these are left unchecked, they start to become automatic and will then govern your behaviour afterwards.

As I approach the Big Wheel with my children, I am saying to myself and out loud to the kids, Isn't this fun? Won't this be great?

Look how strong and safe that Big Wheel looks. Look how much fun other people are having.

You would be amazed how some people come onto our course and during the introductions say things like, 'there is absolutely no way I will be getting on that flight today and there is nothing that you can do about it!' It is one of the most rewarding parts of our job to see people's attitude towards flying completely change by the end of the day to a more positive approach.

Whatever you repeatedly say in your head becomes true for you.

Do you see great sports people looking like they are saying to themselves, 'Goodness me that other athlete looks fitter than me, I bet he wins!'

No they don't.

Once on the dreaded Big Wheel, I keep practicing my deep breathing. I use all the thinking and techniques that are taught on our courses to get me through. I am aware that as I write this, it does not really convey the depth of what we teach people.

I notice my body and if I feel my legs or hands or face tightening, I make them go loose again.

I know that if I can make myself just flop into the chair and keep breathing deeply and saying positive things, I will get through it.

These are some of the techniques we teach people.

A lot of people say, well that sounds easy.

It is - if you practice.

On our courses, we go through what is happening in your mind and how to control it. If it was just as simple as taking deep breaths then we could all do it of course.

19 Are the cheap airlines as safe as the large airlines?

Any airline that flies into UK airspace has to meet the same International Standards that are promoted by the Joint Aviation Authority. This means that they have to meet the same sort of standards that your large airlines like Virgin have to meet.

When the low cost airline business model first appeared, there was a lot of skepticism from the more traditional airlines. They thought that they would never make money.

Clearly this has been shown not to be the case.

It seems crazy that airlines can make money at all. Recently, Richard, one of the Co Founders of this programme, booked very early and managed to fly to Stockholm for the crazy low price of 10 pounds each way.

These airlines do make money though. They make savings in areas that the more traditional airlines do not, such as meals and drinks onboard. By the way, many of the seats even on the cheaper airlines that are booked later can cost hundreds of pounds.

They do not make savings by putting on less fuel or compromising safety. If an airline cut costs by reducing safety measures, they would be grounded by the Civil Aviation Authority in the UK and the equivalent in other countries.

This would appear in the newspapers and no one would fly with them.

We do say this time and time again but it is true. Without safety, there is no business. Safety comes first in all airlines in what you might call the developed world.

We often get asked who it is safe to fly with. We always say that any airline that can fly into the Europe has to meet UK, US, Australia and Asia standards regardless of which country they have come from. If an airline lands and gets spot checked and found to be wanting, it is grounded – simple as that.

In summary, you are just as safe in a low cost airline as you are in a more traditional carrier.

20 When we crash, do my clothes come off?

What a great question and extremely positive of course!

We liked this question because it goes to show how skilled our customers are at imagining disaster!

One particular skill we have noticed that people with a fear of flying have is the ability to imagine their death in intricate detail.

Occasionally, people on our fear of flying courses ask us things like the following:

When we crash, how quickly do we die?

Or

When we crash, do our clothes come off?

Actually, the answer to this question is to look at the question itself.

So, let's examine these questions just for one moment. One of the key statements we tend to emphasize is that, you get more of what you pay attention to.

First of all, the question starts 'WHEN we crash ...'

Using this language is like telling your brain it is a forgone conclusion. Changing it to IF is slightly healthier albeit it is still very very unlikely.

Then, 'How QUICKLY do we DIE?'

This is now telling our brain that not only do we die but it may not be quick - it could be slow.

The answer to this predicament is nothing to do with the answer. It is to do with the question.

We are training our brains to become very good at visualizing death. People without a fear of flying would never allow themselves the luxury of even asking that question. Why would you?

If it is okay to ask that sort of question of ourselves and to tie ourselves up in knots, then we must bring it into other parts of our lives.

For instance, how quickly will I die when I am hit by a bus on the way to work?

How quickly will I die when I crash driving my car today?

Most people don't ask these questions and as you read this you may be saying, 'Of course we don't - that is ridiculous.'

So why does flying get such special attention?

I believe that flying gets a bad rap because it is fairly new. As our captains say on our courses, humans have only been flying for about 100 years really. Humans are not really designed for flying like birds are. It can feel uncomfortable to us as we are not used to weird 3D movement. Our stomachs can lurch occasionally. It is possible for our ears to feel all blocked up. It may also be the only part of your life where you perceive that you have the least amount of control over things. The moment that you arrive at an airport, you could feel like you've become processed as a seat number.

Humans can feel odd in aircraft if they are not used to it. There you go I have said it. It is probably not natural to us with our old fashioned balance organs in our ears. Just because it is uncomfortable it does not mean it is dangerous. Far from it.

Commercial Airlines are so regulated and safe it is staggering.

Everyone that travels in an aircraft, including the pilots, feels the weird sensations of flight. They are just more used to it than everyone else.

The difference between the fearful and the fearless is the interpretation we make of the weird feelings.

The fearful and phobic feel every move of the aircraft and accentuate them. The fearless feel every move of the aircraft and ignore them.

It all comes back to the saying, 'You get what you pay attention to.'

If we dare to allow ourselves to imagine dying and our clothes flying off, we can scare the life out of ourselves. If we practice really hard, we could get really good at it.

It does take practice but if you persevere, you can get yourself to a level of fear whereby just mentioning aircraft can make us come out in a cold sweat. Quite a gift really. Well it would be if we used this particular talent like athletes do.

Picture the scene. 10 athletes line up ready to run the 100 metres. As they look at each other before the event, they visualise the other guy winning. They look at how big his muscles are realise that they probably aren't going to do it today. Today is not THEIR day.

The athletes would never entertain such negative thoughts. They are no different to us. They know that this sophisticated piece of equipment called the brain is so sensitive to every passing thought that they control it.

If they were to think of something negative, they might say STOP to themselves. They would then replace it with images of winning and of getting there first.

If you don't believe me, practice the following guaranteed technique when you are going for your next interview.

Before you go in, say out loud or even just in your head the following mantras:

I don't deserve this job.

The other person is much better suited to it than me.

I look really tired and worn out today.

It probably won't go right today.

Well I think you get the point.

We, at the 'Flying Without Fear' course, are extremely pragmatic about things generally. We would not recommend positive thinking as something other than a very pragmatic way to help yourself. We also recognise positive thinking is not enough on its own - but it is a good place to start.

You really cannot afford the luxury of a negative thoughts because you just get more of what you pay attention to.

21 *Why do the crew get told to sit down sometimes and other times not – do they have special gravity footwear?*

It is safe for them to walk around as they are used to moving with slight turbulence – you are not. The captain ultimately decides when it is safe for passengers and crew to walk around. They have a duty of care towards us all so they will put on the seat belt signs should there be any turbulence. As you know by now, the turbulence has no effect on the aircraft's safety, it is about our comfort. It is very rare that the crew are asked to sit down with the passengers. If it does happen, you are still safe.

22 *I was on a flight and the crew were asked to sit down, is this normally a sign of disaster?*

No, the pilots have a duty of care to the cabin crew as well as to you. If the pilot believes that the turbulence could cause someone to fall over or to spill coffee during a service he/she will suspend the service and ask the crew to sit. This just means a bit too wobbly even for the crew. Like we said before, if you are strapped in, turbulence will cause you no harm whatsoever.

23 *I get worried that I'll try to open the plane door whilst in flight, or that I'll scream or do something to force an emergency landing.*

The doors cannot physically be opened mid-flight and that's a good thing. They are plug type doors which means that they are actually bigger than the hole that they go into. Plus, with the pressure of the Cabin, 10 strong men on the handle could not open it. Also, you'll get to know what cabin crews are trained in to ensure that should someone ever panic, they can assist them.

24 *I am concerned about the length of my flight and the fact it is over water*

First of all, the length of a flight can be worrying for some people as they can imagine it is somehow less safe the longer it is up there. It is safe regardless as the crew have planned for the amount of journey time already. Nothing is left to chance which is why airlines carry so much extra fuel on every flight.

Another thing to consider is this. If the aircraft had enough power to create lift at the beginning of its flight, then as the aircraft has got lighter burning fuel this is even better news for you. For example, if the aircraft could take off easily at 400 tons then by the time it is half way to where it was going, it could be 100 tons lighter. So, if it could get off the ground easily at the beginning of the flight then it still has that extra lift available to it because of being lighter.

Secondly, flying over water is not a problem for the pilots as they always know where they can land at all times. Your flights over water are always on a planned route with more power, more fuel, more diversion airports and more capacity than you will ever need. Incidentally, in the extremely unlikely event that you would need to land on water, all of the crew are trained for this too. Everything has been thought of and planned for on all of your commercial flights.

25 Why don't you put parachutes under the seat instead of stupid life jackets?

The simple truth here is that you are much safer in the air-craft than outside of it, believe it or not. The aircraft crew have been trained to such high levels that there is not any situation that can happen on an aircraft that they have not thought about and prepared for.

David Gott, one of the Senior Cabin Crew Safety Trainers that speaks at our courses, often answers this very question.

David has jumped out of an aircraft for charity. To do that, he received half a day of training. Can you imagine a safety demonstration at the beginning of a flight that lasted one hour?!

Flying is a lot safer than you believe at the moment. Pilots train for every possible eventuality. They know at ALL times the nearest airports to divert to in the unlikely event that they would need to do so. They train for every pos-sible thing that could happen on board an aircraft. Com-mercial pilots are tested every few months on some aspect of their flying abilities. Each of these tests is pass or fail. If they don't make the mark, they lose their licence and that is it for them. This is not an industry where you decide to become a pilot for a bit of a laugh – it is a serious con-templation to get through all the training, testing and then rigorous recruitment.

Dominic Riley, one of our Virgin Atlantic Captains, makes a very simple point about driving versus flying. Once you have passed your driving test at say twenty years of age, no one is interested in testing you again until you get to your seventies. Fifty years of unbridled driving pleasure.

No re-testing. Just you and all those other people on the road driving around at combined speeds of up 140 miles per hour passing within a few feet of each other sometimes.

Up there, it is controlled air space. The pilots are heavily trained and re-tested every six months. The whole industry is heavily regulated on safety grounds like no other.

If we can allow ourselves to think logically, we know it is safer up there than it is down here.

Back to the first question. Why life vests and not parachutes?

There are so many back up systems in place to allow what we call redundancy in the system. Everything has one or two or even more back up systems. People that come on our courses always want to know the worst case scenario.

Here we go.

All the engines failed and we have to land on water.

1. All engines failing is extremely unlikely. It has happened once many years ago due to volcanic ash, which was unknown to affect aircraft then. Even then, the engines came back to life and the aircraft landed normally. Aircraft engines are just incredible. By the way, I found a really terrific website which is **www.rolls-royce.co.uk** where you can look at a modern jet engine being made and be dazzled by their brilliance.

45

2. The aircraft are like big boats. They float. The doors are above the flotation line. The slides that they show in movies are rafts that have more capacity than is possibly needed. Before you ask, this is not a Titanic situation. There are many more spaces than are needed.

3. Can you really imagine leaping confidently out of an aircraft with a parachute with no practice and no idea where you will end up?

In summary, commercial aircraft are incredibly safe. The whole industry is geared to safety. Without safety there is no business.

You are better off with the extremely well trained commercial pilots up there. Aircraft are safe which is why you are better off staying in the aircraft and not go leaping out of it.

26 How can I best prepare for my upcoming flight?

The main piece of advice we would give regarding flying when anxious is preparation.

Maybe this sounds obvious?

The goal of travelling for anyone is to be as prepared as you can be. There was a saying in the military when I served which was that 'you are only as uncomfortable as you want to be'.

This means giving you the best chances possible.

I would divide the preparation into two parts. One is practical and the other is mental.

Mental Preparation

Some readers will say that they don't believe in all this positive thinking mumbo jumbo.

Well, maybe you are right.

However, I ask, is it better to fill your head with positive messages you struggle to believe in or fill it with the latest information from 'Black Box' or 'Crash Files'?

Some people with a fear of flying fill their heads with images of mass destruction. They have had years of practicing watching how they die in their heads. It is quite a skill and takes a lot of practice but if you really apply yourself, you can really imagine the worst death possible!

Imagine someone in the pub told you that they are rubbish at talking in front of people and it always goes badly. You then ask them how to prepare for public speaking?

They reply that they imagine themselves standing up panicking; being lost for words, everyone laughing at them or their clothes falling off in front of the audience!

You would think them crazy to think about all that before and no wonder it does not go well with that mental preparation before hand.

One of the techniques we are trained in is Neuro Linguistic Programming (NLP) and we have a saying that you get more of what you pay attention to. In other words, the more that we think about something going wrong or us not coping with something, the more likely we get just that.

If you mentally practice anything enough times, you get better at it. Why not make your brain work for you instead and turn around the thought process.

You cannot afford the luxury of filling your mind with scary stuff. The more you seek out bad news to confirm that you have every right to keep your fear, the harder you make it for yourself to get over it.

Try an experiment if you'd like some convincing. Don't watch the news, listen to the news or read a newspaper for two weeks. If anyone tells you about some disaster in the public arena, say no thanks.

When your two weeks fast is up, watch the news.

I have tried this and I was shocked by how depressing the news is. 90 per cent of it will be bad news apart from the lighthearted story about the tap dancing Labrador at the end!

The scariest part when I tried this was not how depressing the news is but how easily I switch myself off to it. Bad news becomes the norm because we don't vet what comes into our heads. There has been some research into the 'Bystander effect' when someone witnesses a disaster or accident and that someone does not step in to help. One reason put forward is that we have been desensitized to violence because there is so much on the television.

How does this link to you?

The more you fill your head with the dire, the more you think it is normal.

Aircraft crash very very rarely but when they do it is huge news. They don't crash often enough to justify fearing going on them unless you decide to be scared of every other form of travel too.

'Everyday over 3,500 people are killed on the world's roads and more than 150,000 injured, making this an unending global disaster of vast proportions'

Institute of Advanced Motoring magazine, Winter 2007 edition, UK

Flying is safe.

I think I will now move onto the practical side.

Some top tips around preparing yourself.

- Get everything ready well before hand. Do not leave anything to the last minute. Check passports are in date. Let your airline Special Assistance department know that you are a nervous passenger so they can inform the crew onboard.

- Get to the airport really really early as security is so much tougher now. I would even suggest staying at a hotel the day before so you are nearby and don't have to rush to the airport. When you get to the airport, you can choose whether to join the shouting, rushing frustrated family who don't know where they are going, or simply take your time.

- By the way, someone who worked for the British Airport Authorities, once told me that all their research into passenger behaviour, proved that people don't or can't read airport signs. Passengers become sensory overloaded with all the suspended signs everywhere so they blank them out. In a state of panic, this becomes even worse. Like I say, you can join the mad masses or get there early, learn the layout, get a drink and relax into the environment.

- Wear comfortable clothes. Airports and aircraft are multi temperature zones. Wear what can easily be added to or removed.

- Drink water and lots of it. Air conditioned environments drain you of moisture. The crew are told to drink two litres of water on a flight to counter this. (When you are in the air, this increases the effects of alcohol by two or three times, so be careful.)

- When onboard, move your legs around. Get up and walk around during the flight.

- Look out of the window so that you can keep your sense of perspective. Closing your eyes and clenching strips you of some of your primary human senses that help with balance.

27   *I have had a fear of being sick for the last 15 years and that has interfered in everything I do. When I was younger, I was virtually house bound because of it but as I've aged, I've learned to control the panic attacks etc ... but still won't go on a train, bus, coach, car that I'm not driving, any fairground rides and of course fly.*

We can and regularly do help with fears of having anxiety and panic attacks onboard an aircraft and there are some tips on this in the section of this book around the fear of flying psychology. I would suggest for emetaphobia (fear of being / feeling sick), you contact the National Phobic Society in the UK. They are a fantastic group of people and have experts who can help on this side of things.

28   On Tuesday 13th June 2006 I suffered
      the most horrendous flight courtesy of
      *?!** . The flight was normal and we
      started our descent, its mountainous and
      always a bit bumpy on the way down but
      I'm used to that. We almost got on the
      ground when the aircraft veered violently
      from side to side, up and down. It was
      windy in Almeria but we had landed in the
      same conditions before. Before we knew
      it, the captain gave it full thrust and
      it felt like we were going to the moon,
      all the while the aircraft was swinging
      backwards and forwards and from side to
      side. I looked down and we were clearly
      off course and over houses next to the
      runway, everyone was screaming and crying
      and I honestly thought I was going to
      die. All the while this was happening the
      captain told us nothing until we were
      back up in the air and he said we were
      going to Malaga. His landing at Malaga
      wasn't the greatest in the world but we
      were thankful to be down.

Thank you for your posting. It sounds like you had a rough
time of it to say the least. We can answer what happened
to you but I cannot take away how it felt to you but I can
explain what happened at a factual level.

What you have described as happening to you is something
called a 'Go Around'. It is, believe it or not, a normal procedure. Pilots practice this all the time in the simulator and
it is something that is completely normal to do.

Let me rewind a bit, first of all. When you are coming in to land you have been in the aircraft for a while so your senses are accustomed to the feeling of flying. As you come in, the pilots are flying the aircraft and lining up to land. If they think that there is even the slightest risk to landing because it is too windy or for any other reason, they will abort the landing.

At this moment, you will notice a massive increase in engine power as they put the engine power up positively to effectively take off again. I remember the first time I experienced a 'Go Around' it was quite surprising. The engines had been very quiet and we had the sensation of going down. All of a sudden we were taking off again with a lot of noise. When you don't know what is going on, it can be very alarming. I want you to know that you are in completely safe hands.

The other thing to mention in this very normal procedure is that the pilots are not required to talk to the passengers whilst performing this manoeuvre. That is because their first priority is to fly the aircraft safely. Once the aircraft is back into the landing or holding pattern, they are then free to talk to the passengers. This is all entirely normal. I know it feels very weird but you were not in danger as this is a well practiced procedure.

The thing that we have against us as humans is that we are used to walking around on the Earth. Our inner ear fluids that help us to maintain our balance, struggle to adjust to the movement within aircraft as we cannot always get a sense of horizon since we can't see out the front. Therefore, our sense of whether we are level, leaning forwards or backwards is not accurate. That is a recognized and documented fact. Pilots know this and it is part of their training.

In summary, I am really sorry that you had such an experience. Without knowing exactly what is going on, our brains make sense of what we see and hear and feel. In an aircraft, what we feel is not accurate. A 'Go Around' feels weird and sometimes a little scary but please be assured that it is a normal procedure that all pilots are well trained to cope with.

29   Hello, Recently we have booked a holiday to Ibiza leaving from Manchester and all of a sudden I developed my fear of flying, I've always been a little worried when I have flown before but this time its been a lot worse. I've been thinking about it since it has been booked. I have flown on my own a few times in the last 2 years and have been relatively ok, but now I'm thinking over and over again about what if? All kinds of situations come in to my head from engines blowing up to crashing in water even terrorism. I can't seem to get it out of my head, any advice?

It is not unusual for people's fears to suddenly ratchet up a gear or two. There is not one definitive reason for that to happen. Your brain is very clever and obviously thinks it is time to protect you more from the fear.

Advice I would give is that now is the time to 'nip it in the bud' so to speak. At this point, you are in a position where it is affecting you but not totally stopping you from doing what you want. I would suggest that you get some help now.

30   *Hello—I attended the 2 July Gatwick course, and I was feeling much more confident about my next airplane trip ... But then various American media started making a big deal out of the ten-year anniversary of TWA flight 800; talking about how similar fuel tank problems hadn't been entirely fixed and that another such incident would be "inevitable". Of course, they also said the chances were extremely unlikely (like 1 in a couple of million)*

How does one face media coverage like that and listen to their statistics without reigniting old fears?

Well, there are no quick answers to this. However, if you think about the way that your brain makes connections between events and how it learns things, something very interesting happens.

As you may know, the brain has a neural network that links everything together very quickly. If we can accept that part of our brain function is to protect us, then it is likely that our brain can spot danger or anything linked to danger very quickly.

When our brain sees a pattern in something often enough, it is fair to say that the connections are stronger and quicker.

For instance, you have had a fear of flying for a while so your brain has some really quick and strong connections built up about flying. In effect, you have motorway-like connections that link all the feelings of fear and anything else going on.

Coming on our course, has been like creating a new pathway of thinking when it comes to flying. So compare the two patterns here:

Pattern one (old pattern)	Pattern two (new pattern)
Planes are scary and anything to do with them. We have a super fast motorway linking all the different things to do with being scared.	Planes are safe. We have a dirt track which these thoughts travel on.

Now which would be faster in your car? A motorway or dirt track?

What happens when we hear bad stuff on the telly is that our motorway connections are more likely to be travelled down first. It takes more effort to go on the dirt track! The more times we go down the dirt track, the more pronounced it becomes. In other words, we have to keep reminding ourselves that most of what we hear in the news is wrong. Most of the programmes about aircraft are sensationalised.

We have to keep telling ourselves what we have learned and that is aircraft are the safest form of transport. They are safer than any other way of travelling.

So to conclude, please keep reminding yourself that our business is about safety first. Not every industry works that way. We have to train ourselves to be critical of what we hear on the TV.

31 What happens when the engines fail?

If the engines fail, the aircraft will glide. It is the wing that keeps the aircraft flying. The engines provide thrust and should one or all of them stop working, the aircraft can glide.

32 What if a tyre explodes on landing?

On a 747, there are 18 tyres so nothing would happen to the aircraft. As with everything else in aviation, there are always back up systems in place and more of everything than is needed.

33 Why do the aircraft swing from side to side on landing?

This can often feel a lot worse than it really is because you may be over sensitive to movement due to your fear. The thing to bear in mind is that it is safe and it is under control. The pilot is just making sure that they are completely lined up to land at exactly the right place on the runway. All completely normal and safe.

34 What happens if there is a fire on board?

Cabin crew are trained to deal with fires. It is a big part of their training on which they are assessed pass or fail. We have lots of fire extinguishers onboard and crash axes to get behind panels in the aircraft.

If the fire was in somewhere like the cargo area, there are automatic fire extinguishing systems in there too.

35 Why do the wings flap up and down?

The wing tips can move up to 12 feet in some aircraft and they are meant to do that. They are made of extremely strong yet flexible metal and they act like a suspension system. When the aircraft is manufactured, they test all of its components to destruction so that they can understand how long its flying life will be. The wings are pulled up with huge hydraulics to see when they would reach their ultimate load. A vast safety margin is then built into the proposed lifespan of the aircraft. People often worry about this because they believe that the wings will just fall off. They are not just bolted on, they are an integral part of the aircraft and cannot snap off.

36 *I have read your top 10 reasons* people are afraid to fly. The only one that bothers me at all is the fear of crashing. Does this happen very often?*

The straight answer is not very often at all. It can seem more because we hear about every single aircraft that crashes anywhere in the world and that includes light aircraft, commercial and non-commercial, flown by inexperienced pilots. It is news worthy because it makes for some great dramatic headlines.

We always talk about reality on our courses and we are honest. Aircraft hardly ever crash, but knowing that fact is not enough for you to conquer your fear. We all know that we could die in lots of ways but the least likely way is travelling by commercial aircraft. It really is the only business that puts safety first. When we talk about flying on our courses, we are talking about commercial flying. All commercial aircraft that you will fly on will be flown by experts, not someone with less experience such as just a private pilot's licence.

The most dangerous part of people's holidays are:

- Crossing the road to get into your car.

- Getting in your car and driving to the airport.

- Walking through the car park at the airport.

- Getting on the coach at your destination.

These are the bits that will more likely lead you to harm than flying on an aircraft.

*Top ten reasons why people fear flying is a free report that we issue with our newsletters. The content has been covered in this book.

37   *I'm sorry to go over and over the same subjects but I fly in 9 days time and am seriously considering cancelling – it takes a lot to keep positive when you keep hearing conflicting reports. Can lightning, thunderstorms, turbulence really bring a plane down? If not, why does the press keep reporting it like this? I hope you can once again put me at ease. Many thanks in anticipation of your response.*

We have spoken with three pilots independently about this and it has confirmed what we knew.

The news that is being released is at best inaccurate at worst ridiculous. Aircraft do not burst into flames when hit by lightning. Turbulence is uncomfortable but is not dangerous to the aircraft. Don't let the news put you off your good work. I really do recommend that you stop watching anything from the news about flying because it is not always 100% accurate. If you really want to know something put a message on our message board and we will answer for you.

38   *Hello, I have only just discovered this site [www.flyingwithoutfear.info] and have really found it very friendly and informative.*
I seem to suffer from every one of the main fears that you outline on your site!
I even worry about little things that most people don't consider like what would happen if that cabin air supply failed? I haven't flown in years but I was convinced on my last flight that I felt dizzy due to the lack of oxygen. I'm also afraid if what everyone tells me is true, that long haul flights are in fact boring, doesn't that mean that the pilot will feel bored and complacent? I lose concentration every day at work, why shouldn't he??
One last major fear, I used to work in various car dealers, the technicians are only human after all and often used to come to work on a Monday morning with a hangover?? Or having some personal trauma that meant their mind wasn't on the job. Little mistakes were common place. Airline technicians are human too!! Why should they be incapable of mistakes????

- The cabin pressure is set to about 6,000 feet which is like a mountain top. It is very comfortable for humans to operate at that altitude. Sometimes people report feel a little bit breathless. The crew often report it when they are working a lot and not feeling as fit as they should. All airlines carry oxygen onboard so if you want a top up, so to speak, it is available.

- The pilots getting bored could happen if they were on their own. However, the pilots job is to monitor the controls and constantly plan for 'what ifs' so they are alert. There are always at least two and sometimes more depending on how long the flight is. They check on each other. The cabin crew check on them regularly to see they are okay.

- The pilots and cabin crew are not allowed to drink or do anything that is going to compromise their position as they will lose their jobs. Most people can go into work and risk being a bit sleepy or hung-over or even rough. Not pilots. They check on each other and if one of them is feeling rough or has had domestic problems, they have full permission from the Chief Pilot to say, 'I am not flying today.' There are always standby pilots to step in to take the flight instead. They are not prepared to lose their livelihood and jobs due to having a bad day.

- Technicians for airlines are certificated and their training is intensive and thorough too. They are checked and every nut and bolt is checked every time the aircraft lands. There is no room for sloppiness within airlines. The captain will not sign off an aircraft to fly unless he or she is completely happy that everything is in order.

39 *What happens if we land in the sea?*

You will be pleased to know that the pilots practice this in the simulators. The cabin crew are trained and tested on this. The doors, if opened once they have been 'put to automatic or armed' will automatically inflate slide rafts. They are dual purpose slides for a ground landing and rafts for a sea landing. All aircraft have to be able to float and they do.

40 *What happens if the pilot has had an argument with his/her partner the night before and is in the wrong mood to fly?*

The pilots are too responsible for that to happen. The reason behind two pilot flights is that they can check each other. All pilots are trained to challenge each other. If one pilot thought that the other one was not fit to fly, they would do exactly that. The pilot, with no prejudice from the company, would be given leave there and then. One of the pilots on standby would then be called out to cover the flight. A slight delay possibly to the passengers would be the worst that is going to happen.

41 *When I flew last week there was what looked like smoke pouring along the ceiling as we were waiting to taxi up the runway, what was this as it didn't smell smokey? Also I always get a cold or the flu after flying. Are airplanes germ breeding grounds or is it just coincidence?*

In answer to your smokey looking stuff in the cabin but no smoke smell, that is the air conditioning units. When they start up sometimes they throw out white condensation mist before it goes clear. It happens in my car if I have not used the air conditioning for a while - all perfectly normal. It can be alarming if you don't know that though.

Next question about Germ breeding grounds. This did make me smile because I seem to get colds when I go away. I have several theories on this.

The air onboard aircraft is changed all the time from outside. It is quite cold in aircraft which can make you feel a bit fluey. It could be that you are feeling run down thinking about the flight and have not slept properly.
It could be that you are now on holiday and now your immune system thinks, 'Great no more work, now let's rebuild the body and ensure she takes proper rest.'

The last thing is that if you go anywhere with a lot of people there is always a chance of picking up a bug. Ever been to a concert and then picked up a cold couple of days later?

42   As a nervous flyer I would like to ask a question about turbulence and clouds. I am not sure whether I have experienced turbulence or not, or what it really is. Many years ago I flew on a TU88 from Manchester to Leningrad (as it was then). The steward had just passed me a tray with a meal on it when the aircraft suddenly felt as if it was going to drop out of the sky - there was an awful sinking feeling. I opened my mouth to scream but it never came out, as the next minute the aircraft "came up again" - like a lift. I shut my mouth quickly and passed the tray back to the steward,

*as I had suddenly lost my appetite. I
was sick with fright for the rest of the
flight. Was that turbulence?
I have flown since but I am still very
nervous. I have noticed that when the
aircraft passes through clouds it seems
to shudder. Why is this?*

The chances are that it was turbulence if you understand that turbulence just means movement of air. The air is always moving around and the aircraft fly through it. Just as a boat on a river moves about with the currents, aircraft do the same. When you feel like the aircraft is dropping, it feels like it is dropping but it is not. It is travelling anything up to 500 miles an hour so, the air moving over the wings changes pressure, it will cause the aircraft to move up and down. As we can't see outside properly, our poor inner ear fluids struggle to make sense of what is happening and over accentuate what is really going on (in the absence of other visual cues we can't really tell how much we move). Our ear fluids which keep us balanced struggle to work out what is going on and then send us duff messages about how far we have moved within the air. This is covered really clearly on our courses.

Clouds are formed because the columns of air and temperature at that precise point has reached condensation point. This means that the water vapour that is always present in air (but normally invisible) has condensed out into a visible cloud. Since pressure and temperature affect lift the aircraft will 'wobble' slightly at the moment of cloud entry until the local air pressure over the wing has stabilized. There may also be local air currents that have affected the cloud formation. These too will provide slight turbulence through which the aircraft must fly.

43 *One of the things I have heard is on landing, you get a tickle sensation in your stomach which is one of the reasons I won't go on fairground rides, because I don't like it. Also my stomach is quite sensitive to things like this and I know if I go on the course and this happens, it will be the one and only time I do it. Is this true??*

It is true to some degree that you get weird bodily sensations sometimes. None of which are dangerous to us though. The main thing to think about is that your body does have some awareness of movement within the aircraft and sometimes that may feel odd to folk. The main thing that I would say it is a bit like going over a small hump back bridge. If you have even done that, you are aware of a slight sinking feeling in your stomach. All quite harmless once you know what is going on. That is the thing. You may well feel slightly peculiar bodily sensations but none of them are dangerous to you. It is about what you tell your-self about these sensations. If you know that these things happen and that they are normal, and most importantly, every human experiences them; then you can rationalise them.

44 *Why should I trust a pilot that I do not know?*

You are correct in that you do not know the pilot and this can be a worry for some people. The pilots that fly commercial aircraft have invested a significant amount of money into their career to get themselves flying in the first place. Right now, at the time of writing, it can cost £80,000 to get trained. Once they have passed all their training, it does not guarantee a job at all. They still have to go through a very rigorous recruitment. Then, they are on probation to make sure that they are the right type of person for the job. This is a highly regulated industry unlike any other.

Don't forget that pilots also have mortgages to pay, loved ones to go home to just like you. They are not some form of daredevils as sometimes depicted in Hollywood.

45 Why do I feel closed in when I fly?

Aircraft can feel closed in for some people. They are not for others though. The reason why you might feel closed in is particular to you. One of the main reasons that our customers tell us is linked to the door closing. With other forms of transport, it does seem that you can get out when you want to. Even with boats where you can't get off very easily, you can go out onto the decks.

Despite what you might think, aircraft are extremely safe to be in. They are so regulated for safety reasons. The air is changed all the time and they are as comfortable as you want to be. You need to find a strategy to help with that feeling. It is about learning to feel comfortable when you are not in the environment so that you can learn to do it later. One of the things that we talk about later in the book is around the research of Wolpe. He experimented successfully with something called counter conditioning or nowadays called gradual desensitisation. He found that by combining the relaxation response with a small amount of the feared thing, that you can gradually overcome the fear response. In other words, you gradually put yourself into your feared situation to get used to it. If it was tube journeys, this would mean visiting them regularly and doing a little bit more each time whilst practising deep breathing. This, over time, starts to change your automatic response to the fear. It works and it is being spoken about a lot in fear of flying circles at the moment.

46 What is that funny sinking feeling just after take off?

Around 1,500 feet after take off, any humans travelling in an aircraft will notice a slight sinking feeling. This is the point when the pilots change their power settings to reduce the noise signature near airports. This is regulated world wide so you will always feel it every time you fly. It is normal. The reason that we notice it is that humans are very reliant upon our eyes to get a sense of balance and motion. In an aircraft, you are not able to see out the front so the balance organs in your ear start to work overtime. You will notice the pitch of the aircraft on take off as a more severe angle than it actually is. Then your ears stabilise quite quickly after that. Then, the pilot changes the angle of the aircraft at 1,500 feet while still climbing and you will feel it as the nose is slightly lowered. It will only be a couple of degrees in pitch but to our basic human systems, it can feel a lot greater than it is. Of course, just to help you, the pilots also reduce the engine noise slightly and maybe bring in the flaps on the wings at the same time. All of this, combined, when you don't know what is going on, can make you feel unsure and you may start to fill in the gaps in your knowledge with what you think is happening rather than what is happening.

The pilots also feel this sensation but they can see out of the front plus, they are trained to expect this bodily sensation and to rely on their instrumentation.

The sinking could also be when you are sitting in the rear of the aircraft. As the rear of the aircraft pivots down slightly before taking off, you may notice it. It is normal and not everyone feels it.

47   What is wind shear?

This is when the local air currents are moving in different directions at very similar heights. If these currents are slow speed then there is nothing to worry about. Similarly at 30,000 feet there is nothing to worry about. But, if these air currents are at 10-30 miles per hour different to each other and the aircraft is either taking off or coming in to land, then a significant situation is present. No aircraft can safely cope with a sudden reduction of 30 mph in its forward speed so close to the ground. Therefore, commercial aircraft are fitted with a Doppler wind shear detection system. Also, any airfield that is susceptible to windshear is also equipped with sophisticated detection devices. But as with all things, it might be safer to either not take off or divert if necessary.

48   Where is the safest place to sit?

It is safe to sit anywhere on an aircraft. There are lots of myths around flying such as:

- The brace position, of placing your head down to your knees for emergency landings is the quickest way to break your neck!

- The rear or the aircraft is most likely to break off first so if you sit at the front it will most likely stay intact – that is why the seat prices cost more!

I am pleased to tell you that such stories are wrong.

The aircraft really is safe anywhere. It is all about prefer-ence seating wise. Some people like to sit up the front as it is slightly quieter as you are forward of the engines. Some prefer to sit next to the wing as there is slightly less move-ment than the rest of the aircraft (some like it because they can keep checking the engines!)

It really does not matter where you sit in terms of safety.

49   What happens if the plane is too heavy for take off?

This can't happen as the pilots have already worked out the weight before takeoff. They know exactly what the weight is and will have worked out what speed they need to achieve for takeoff. They will have also worked out the length of runway needed to take off and will have more than enough fuel and energy to achieve it. Safety margins are built into everything. These calculations are double checked. The pilots work out the correct takeoff speed into which a safety margin is built. Any change to the weight of weather will require a re-calculation. Always – safety first.

50   Why do aircraft crash?

Commercial airlines in the developed world have very few incidents of note. They are so regulated around safety, the chances are minute. Most of the incidents that you hear about are private pilots or aircraft in places that you haven't heard of. This is not meant to be glib at all. Incidents are incredibly rare which is why they are news.

The other point to re-enforce that came up earlier was that whenever something happens in the aviation industry, everyone knows about it. If there was found to be small widget that needed changing on the 747 – 400, every airline that operated that aircraft type would receive a mandate to change it immediately. The point is that the airline industry learns from anything that happens and shares the learning.

51 Why does the aircraft creak so much on landing?

All aircraft have been designed to do that. They are not rigid even the wings are meant to move up and down. It is the flexibility that gives them strength. The overhead storage bins and similar within the cabin itself are made to flex and move about. So, all the noises are normal even if you don't like the sound of them.

52 I had water fall on me when sat by a window, was that a leak?

The air-conditioning vents are positioned along the cabin. When the air conditioning units are turned on after a period of being off, they sometimes produce water as a by-product of the cooling, just like your car would. All completely normal.

53 Why doesn't the aircraft just roll over when it turns?

The reason that the aircraft does not just roll over is that you have professional pilots flying them. The 747 has enough awesome power that it can be rolled over, fly upside down and then fly normal again – without passengers I hasten to add. The Airbus fleet of aircraft have a computer inhibitor built in which prohibits more than 67% bank.

54 What about second hand spares?

This just does not happen. All of the spares have to be bought from recognised and agreed suppliers because they have to be stressed to 6 million to 1 against failure. Safety is too important for airlines to risk it by buying suspect spares from e-Bay! All of the parts have to be recognised, accounted for, and fitted by a certified engineer. The engineer also has his or her work signed off too by a supervising engineer.

55 What about radio failures?

There are back up systems of absolutely everything on aircraft. Most commercial aircraft have up to five separate radios as well as a satellite phone.

56 When we were allowed into the flight deck, I went in and the pilot was reading a newspaper.

That may well have happened. There are always at least two pilots. The other pilot would have been managing the sophisticated flying apparatus. It has also been proven that if the pilots are doing something like reading newspapers and crosswords for instance, it keeps them nicely alert. You would never have found them settling down with a pipe and a good book – they are permanently on duty and take that very seriously.

57 We were diverted for a bit of wind one day – why is that?

All aircraft have a legal crosswind limit for take offs and landings. If the wind exceeds this limit, the pilot is prohibited from making a landing and will divert to a more suitable runway or, wait in the holding pattern away from the airfield until the wind changes.

58 *What happens if the pilot has a heart attack on take off?*

The pilots are constantly cross checking with each other. If one pilot died, the other would simply carry on the take off – that is what they are trained to do. Cabin crew are trained to come in, remove the pilot and help them with their medical training that they receive. The aircraft would then land at the first most suitable airfield.

59 *What happens if the pilot does not speak Mandarin when flying over China?*

The international language is English which all air traffic controllers use worldwide. If a Chinese air traffic control is talking to a pilot from Air China, she might speak Mandarin. If there is another pilot listening in on an open frequency who doesn't speak Mandarin, they will repeat the message in English.

60 *Why so many near misses these days?*

This is not the case. There are huge safety margins around every aircraft in the sky right now. If one aircraft breaks these safety margins, it will be noticed by the pilots and air traffic control. If this happens, it has to be logged as an incident. All modern aircraft are fitted with Traffic Collision Avoidance Systems that talk to each other. So, if you are in aircraft A on the same possible course as aircraft B, you will both get a warning of what to do to avoid each other. One will be advised to go up and the other go down. It is a great piece of equipment and commercial aircraft are not allowed to take off if it is not working.

71

61 What happens if I become ill on board?

The cabin crew are extremely well trained in Aviation Medicine. They can deal with anything from a faint to childbirth. There are first aid kits on board which are jam packed with bandages, paracetamol, plasters, eyewash and all sorts. There is also a Doctor's medical kit which contains lots of drugs that only a medically qualified person can administer. On Virgin aircraft we also carry a defibrillator which can re-start the heart. Every airline also carries extra oxygen. If you are planning to be ill, there is no better place for it to happen as the crew know that they have to be able to deal with anything that could happen up there. That is why the crew are trained so thoroughly. Please see David Gott's section later on in this book for more information.

62 What would you do if I had a panic attack?

Dealing with Panic Attacks is part of the cabin crew Aviation Medical Training. Crew will calm you down by talking to you calmly and helping you to get your breathing back to normal. This helps the panic attack to subside as it is impossible to be hyperventilating if you are calm. The crew will also establish what triggered the attack and then help in whatever way that they can. Please remember, cabin crew do the job because they like working with people. They like to help and when someone is upset, they will do whatever they can to make them happy again. Also, it is worth mentioning here, that if you are prone to panic attacks, please tell the airline before hand. Virgin Atlantic has a Special Assistance department that will put a note in your booking so that the ground staff and cabin crew know that you may need some extra help.

63 *What happens if the pilot is having a bad day?*

Pilots are extremely professional people. They also fly with another pilot as a minimum. If the other pilot thought that their colleague seemed under the weather, they would suggest that they did not fly. There are always stand by pilots should someone need to come off a flight. Plus, it does not go against the pilot if they don't feel fit to fly.

64 *Why are the lights dimmed at night for take off?*

In the unlikely event of an evacuation, the lights are dimmed so that your eyes are adjusted in case you need to leave the aircraft quickly.

65 *Why do the window blinds have to be up for take off and landing?*

As above, this helps everyone to adjust their eyes to the outside conditions. Should you need to evacuate from the aircraft, the cabin crew need to be able to see outside clearly before they open the door. This is to prevent opening a door and there being something outside that obstructs your exit.

66 *What is the call bell noise which means we are about to crash?*

There is no such code. If anything happens on board that you need to know about for either your safety or comfort, you will be told. There is no conspiracy and call bells are only used for routine things for the crew to do such as sit down for take off. IF anything happened you would be told.

67 What happens if the engine catches fire during the flight?

All of the engines have their own fire extinguishers that would be activated. Also, the fuel would be turned off as you need three elements to have fire which are heat, oxygen and combustible material. Turning the fuel off removes the obvious material. In most cases, the flame would simply blow out due to the speed that the aircraft is travelling at. The aircraft can then either continue on to its destination or return.

68 I have noticed that people are getting heavier and we are not weighed at the airport - how can it be safe?

This question of weight has been raised on a lot of our courses. There is also a linked concern around the amount of baggage that people bring onto aircraft.

Let us put your mind at ease here.

The pilots know exactly how much the aircraft weighs when it takes off. There are load sheets which tell the captain what weight cargo and suitcases are. On a lot of aircraft, there are weight indicators in the wheels so they know exactly what the weight is.

All of your bags are weighed as you know.

The passengers are not weighed as they don't need to be - which is probably just as well with the delays that could cause.

A man and a woman are given a nominal weight each. For example, for a man it is 85KG (at time of writing). This works out because some men will be over that and some will be under. By the way, this average weight allowance has gone up over the years!

So, the aircraft loaders know exactly what the dry weight of the aircraft is. They know how much fuel they load. They know the weight of the baggage that goes on. All of the passengers are counted and bags matched up. The captain checks the load sheet and signs it before the aircraft takes off.

So, the next time you are checking in at an airport and see massive bags, do not worry. All of it will be accounted for before your aircraft departs.

69 What happens if a lunatic tries to open the door?

There are two very important points to make here. First of all, if anybody tried to open the door in flight it won't open. Once the aircraft takes off, the pressurisation of the cabin begins. This creates huge pressure on each door. As the doors are bigger than the hole that they are in, it is impossible to open them. When the doors are not pressurised, they are guarded by a member of cabin crew – basically, when you are boarding the aircraft and when you going down the runway.

The next point to make here is that if anybody was to behave in what the crew perceived as a dangerous manner, they will intervene. Virgin Atlantic Crew are trained in restraint techniques and as a last resort would use the restraint straps we carry on every aircraft. The captain would also radio ahead to have Police meet the aircraft. Please remember, the crew are very adept at talking to people and reassuring all sorts of people from all around the world.

The bottom line is that the cabin crew would contain the situation.

70   Why don't all aircraft have four engines?

Modern engines are extremely reliable and the aircraft are built with the right amount of engines that they need for the weight and size of the aircraft. As engine technology and reliability increases, the engines are now much more powerful. For instance, the engines on the Boeing 777 (Two engine aircraft) are huge and the 777 is as long as a Jumbo 747!

71   How do Gliders stay up without engines?

Gliders stay up because of the skilful way that their wings are made to support flight. They only need energy to get up there which is normally either they are towed up or catapulted. The wing is so elegantly designed that they can maintain flight for hours with no engines simply by glid-ing downhill at a very shallow angle. Indeed if the glider pilot can locate a warm air thermal of rising air he can glide uphill! Remember, it is the wing that provides lift. Commer-cial aircraft are like huge gliders and the engines are needed for take off and to help us to arrive at the location that we bought a ticket for.

72   Do you need engines for landing?

No. Pilots are trained to land without engines as essentially, they are huge gliders. If an aircraft was to come in with no engines, air traffic control would completely clear the air space so that the pilots could achieve the best approach. It is something that the pilots practice in the simulator.

73 *On a two engined aircraft and one engine fails, why don't we fly around in circles?*

The pilots would use the huge rudder to offset this happening. This would enable the aircraft to fly normally albeit it would not be 100% straight. This is much like a boat's rudder would compensate for a failed propeller on a two propeller boat.

74 *Do you use full power for take off?*

All commercial aircraft use enough power to enable the take off to be performed with suitable safety margins. This will always depend on the type of aircraft, the weight of the aircraft and the length of the runway among other things. Most of the noise is at the top of the power range so that is what makes the take off sound so exciting.

75 *Someone told me that when you land into Heathrow, pilots glide in with the engines off – is that true?*

No, but when coming to into an airport, for about 100 miles before landing, the engines are put into idle from our cruising height of about 35,000 feet. This means that they are there if needed but not providing much power to the aircraft as it is not needed – remember they glide!

The engines could potentially stay on this setting but this does not happen because the air traffic controllers will somtimes be asking us to change settings, levelling, descending etc which is why you will hear the engines getting louder and quieter all the way into landing. All perfectly normal and just know that the pilots are actively managing the flight all the way down. As they are busy doing this, you may not get as many announcements over the P.A. during this time.

76 What does 'Doors to Automatic and Cross Check' mean?

This command is given to the cabin crew once all of the passengers have boarded and all the doors are shut. The cabin crew will then move a small lever within the door and this makes the door ready to use should you need to evacuate. If you were to open the door now, the slide/raft will come out from the underneath the door. That is why, once this happens, you will never see a door unattended on the ground. Obviously, once you are airborne, you can't open the doors anyway.

77 How often are aircraft serviced?

Every time an aircraft lands it is crawled over by engineers. The servicing schedules are set by the manufacture and they have to be adhered to. This is decided on the number of landings the aircraft will make, the number of hours airborne. The checks on an Airbus A-340 which flies to Hong Kong and Japan most of its life will be different to a 737 that flies to Edinburgh and back every day. The main comfort to take from here is that it is heavily regulated and the checks have to be done. This is standard across all airlines regardless of how cheap your ticket may have been. Safety is an area in which compromises cannot be made.

78 I have seen that the low cost carriers take off after 20 minutes on the ground does that mean they are not checked as well?

They are all still as thoroughly checked as they need to be. They will have all their fluid levels checked in that time. The aircraft will have a longer check after it has done more sectors. Again, this is decided at the point of manufacture so has to be followed. It is completely regulated and safe.

79 I have heard that you can't land in fog – is that true?

Most modern airlines are now equipped with autopilots capable of landing the aircraft safely in visibility down to 75 metres. However, the airfield must also be suitably equipped. Not all are. Heathrow, Gatwick, Glasgow, Birmingham, Stansted, Manchester, Newcastle, Edinburgh and East Midlands in the UK are all equipped for this.

80 Why does the pilot make it as wobbly as turbulence when you are about to land?

The pilots are getting the aircraft lined up to make the best approach and landing that they can. It does involve a little bit of jiggling around to get it just right. A bit like you going into a car parking space, you take it slowly and make adjustments as you go in to get it just right.

81 I have heard pilots don't land aeroplanes any more.

It is possible for some aircraft to land themselves. This is used in fog for instance as the aircraft does not need to be able to see. Rest assured, this is completely safe and the pilots are monitoring the whole time that it happens. Should they not be happy with the approach, the pilots can override the automatic landing. It is incredibly safe as computers can react quicker than humans can.

82 Can you land in cross winds?

Yes you can. There are legal limits as to what those cross winds speed can be which is detected by monitors on the airfield.

83 How can it still be safe with all the extra air traffic now?

It is safe. The safety margins don't change and as you would expect, air traffic is highly regulated and controlled too.

84 How do you know when to divert when someone is seriously ill?

This is a joint decision between the cabin crew dealing with the passenger and the captain. The captain will also be getting advice from the Medlink service that is mentioned in David Gott's notes later in this book.

85 I was stopped with a bottle of mineral water going through security - why is that ridiculous system in place?

When you fly now, you will be subjected to extremely thorough security checks. Part of the security measures in place include stopping anything coming from outside bigger than 100ml. (at time of writing). This includes deodorant, water, shaving foam etc. All pastes and lipsticks have to be screened separately too.

Once you are through security, you can buy water for the flight. The items that you buy after security have already been screened so are known to be safe.

If you want to take large bottles of perfume or anything like that, put it in your suitcase as that is screened separately many times plus, you would not have access to it onboard the flight which makes the cabin safer. Please don't take anything through security that you know is going to be bigger than 100 ml (at the time of writing) as it will taken from you. This is all done to ensure our safety and that is the thought to keep in mind. Please check your airport website for up to date information on what you can take with you.

86 Why are aircraft so claustrophobic?

Aircraft are the size that they need to be to fit the people that go in them. People seem to have different reactions to the aircraft size. I am thinking of our customers that have never flown and when they first look into the cabin, what they report. Most say it seems a lot bigger than they thought it would be.

The reality is that if you are travelling in Economy, there is not as much space as in Upper class. This does not mean it is any less safe. If aircraft genuinely seem closed in to you, then that is what you need to address when you come onto our courses.

It is all about what you think of the space. If you are convinced it is closed in, then you will perceive it to be. Humans that go into the same space as you will perceive it differently. Some might agree that they feel a bit cramped but not all will believe it is claustrophobic. It is about the thought patterns that go on in our minds. There are some tips that are in the psychology section at the back of this book.

87 *Does the captain put the seat belt sign on so the cabin crew can do the service more easily?*

The pilots put the seat belts signs on for you as a duty of care towards you. They will not put them on just to help the crew do the service.

88 *Why don't the pilots talk to us more during the flights*

The pilots main role is to fly the aircraft safely which they do. They are also given certain times that they should talk to the passengers such as welcome, prior to landing and if anything happens that they feel passengers should know about, such as a diversion to another airport. Some pilots really enjoy talking to passengers whilst others do not feel as comfortable. Please be assured that it is in no way a reflection upon their abilities as a pilot.

89 *If I have a panic attack, can someone just sedate me?*

We would not do that. There are lots of other ways to talk you down from a panic attack. One of the easiest ways for crew is to help you to stop hyperventilating which is common with panic attacks.

90 *I feel more out of breath up there – is that the airline trying to save money?*

The airlines do not scrimp on money by putting less air in the cabin. The air is constantly being changed and don't forget the cabin crew are breathing the same air as you are.

91 What happens if the wheels don't come up after take off?

The wheels weigh several tons and need huge hydraulic systems to lift them. There are always back up systems of course. If nothing works, the pilots will land back where they took off most likely. There is no danger to us as the wheels are already down. The pilots will lose some fuel to lighten the aircraft and then land again. Before you ask, the aircraft can land at exactly the same weight as when it took off if needs be.

92 What happens if the wheels don't come down when you are coming into land?

Again, this is something that is extremely rare. We hope that by now that you are beginning to realise that there are back up systems for everything onboard the aircraft? This is no exception. There are various ways to bring the wheels down and please remember that the wheels are actually held UP. They weigh tons so want to lower with gravity. Worse case scenario, the aircraft can land without any wheels whatsoever. It might not be very comfortable but it can be done.

93 Aren't most accidents just due to pilot error now?

In the 1950s most accidents were aircraft related. The sophistication of modern aircraft over the last 20 or so years has meant that things rarely go wrong with aircraft now. The weak link in the chain is the human, as it is in a lot of jobs. The airlines recognise this which is why so much money is put into Human Factors Training to reduce the possibility of error. This approach to understanding why humans do bizarre stuff is also being adopted by other crucial jobs such as operating surgeons. The pilots are constantly cross checking with each other. Nobody presses a button or does anything until they have checked with each other first.

94 What happens if the engine stalls?

A jet engine requires a smooth flow of air into the first stage of the compressor blades (the ones that are just behind the ones you can see when you look at an engine from the front). If this airflow is disrupted, the engine may stall. It's not like when a car stalls and the engine stops, it's more of a splutter – think of it as a bit like you were choking. As soon as the airflow is restored, all is well again as the engine will function normally.

If the wing stalls, it means that the airflow has broken away from the upper surface of the wing and the lift has been lost. Not a good thing, but will not happen in a commercial aircraft due to the safety devices incorporated into the flying controls. Aerobatic aircraft, fighter jets and small civilian aircraft might be affected due to nature of their smaller flying characterisation.

95 Why do the pilots hold back information from us?

Pilots will always tell you what you need to know if it will affect you. They will not tell you that widget C on flange bracket B has gone if it makes no difference to your flight or safety. If you were woken up by the captain's voice telling about some pointless problem that does not make any difference to anything, I am sure that you would sit there worrying unnecessarily for the remainder of the flight.

96 *What happens if the pilot gets tired?*

The pilot hours are extremely regulated from the time that they leave home until they land. Every thought is put into their rosters to make sure that they get the right rest. When they work, they always work in a minimum of pairs and on the longer flights there can be anything up to four pilots. There is also a crew bunk behind the flight deck where they can get proper rest.

97 *My fear did not start till I had children –why is that?*

No-one quite knows why this is the case but we do know that it is a common trend amongst our customers. One of our theories is around responsibility. It is a huge increase in responsibility just having children as it is. All of a sudden you are responsible for another person's life. This can weigh heavily on parents and carers. Going through an airport and checking in and then flying are when, quite rightly, you are least in control of what happens to you. All of these factors can trigger the fear in someone, which often comes as a huge surprise to the recipient themselves.

98 *How do pilots see through clouds when we can't?*

Pilots fly using instrumentation. They are tested on the ability to fly in the dark and through clouds and fog using instruments alone. In fact, even on clear days, they still use their instruments to double check because of the weird sensations that our human balance organs throw up for us anyway. Dark, clouds and fog make no difference to the aircraft. It does not know whether it is day or night.

99 *What happens if the window cracks?*

This is very unlikely. If a crack went undetected, the aircraft would slowly depressurise which the Pilots would be able to detect and then take action. Such as bringing the aircraft down to a level where we can breathe normally. Plus, as soon as the pressure dropped, the oxygen masks would come down so we would be safe.

100 *Would we really survive if we crash landed onto the sea?*

First of all, the aircraft can land onto the sea without having to crash. This is something that the pilots have to practice in the simulator. The aircraft are air filled tubes so will float. The crew train for this and there are plenty of life rafts onboard for people to get into.

101 *When we take off, it sometimes feels like we are going too steeply and we could fall backwards - why?*

You can't fall backwards as you always have thrust pushing forward and you have already achieved lift over the wings. Also, as we mentioned before, your brain will be giving you false signals about your actual angle of take off and climb. It is only likely to be about fourteen degrees of pitch but you could feel this like a rocket shooting upwards! Your brain is used to walking around on the ground. We have not evolved enough yet to be totally comfortable with 3D movement like birds are. Just because it is uncomfortable does not make it dangerous. You do not have to love flying like we do, but know that it is incredibly safe.

Also, some of you may worry about the tail hitting the ground as you take off. The tail won't hit the ground due to the skill of the pilots. Also, some aircraft have little rubber bumpers on the bottom of the tail to prevent scraping.

In Summary.

The commercial aviation industry is all about safety. Everything has been thought about and planned for. The aircraft can do a lot more than we will ever need it to do. There is spare capacity built into every part of the aircraft and its systems – nothing is ever left to chance. The pilots that fly your aircraft are better trained than you can imagine. The aircraft have been tested to limits that they will never approach on any commercial flight. It is the safest form of transport and it is an industry where safety really does come first before anything else. Believe not a word you hear from others or read in the papers, flying IS safe.

Top Tips From Aviation Experts

The Aircraft

Aircraft used in Public transport are extremely safe and reliable. They have to meet safety standards that have been developed over many years. These standards have to be much higher than those found in any other form of public transport.

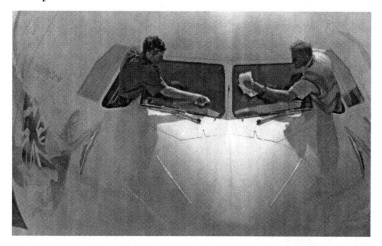

If your car had to be as safe or well constructed it would be too expensive for us to buy!

So, how can such a large object fly? How does it stay up there? We will now look at all the different parts of the aircraft so that you can understand what is going on. With knowledge comes power; with power comes control as David Landau our psychotherapist would say.

The Wing

Contrary to what you might think, wings are built and the aircraft rests on them. They are built in a way that they become one piece. The parts of the wing that we can see are shaped to form what Bernoulli called an aerofoil. This means in normal speak that the top half of the wing is curved slightly more than the bottom half. Therefore, any air that passes over the wing has to go slightly further over the top than the air travels that goes under the wing. This is key to flying as we will come onto.

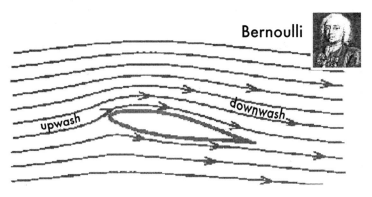

Bernoulli

The air travelling over the top surface has to travel further and because of this it has to travel faster to meet the air coming under the wing shape. This is physics – it just happens. Bernoulli was extremely pleased when he discovered this but unfortunately did not know what to do with the information otherwise we would have had aircraft flying sooner! Now there's a thought as our Captain Dominic would say.

> Imagine Richard is one air molecule and Judy is the other. As they approach the aerofoil shape, they get separated. They want to get back together at the other side as quickly as possible of course. Now Richard went over the top of the curve and Judy went under. As the curve at the top was more curved than the bottom therefore Richard had further to go, Richard has to go faster to make sure he is there to meet Judy at the same time. This is what Bernoulli discovered.

If the air travelling over the upper surface goes faster to meet the air under the wing shape, it causes a reduction in pressure. This means that the pressure underneath the wing is now greater than the pressure over the wing. The wing and everything attached to it (the aircraft, the cabin crew, you) will now rise. That is physics. There is lots of empirical data to measure this which we won't cover here but that's it. That is LIFT. The pressures seek to equalize. The higher pressure below the wing seeks to equalize with the lower pressure above the wing.

Lift is one of the factors that pilots manage. The wings are made big enough to produce the amount of lift needed for the size of aircraft attached to it. In theory there is no limit to the size of an aircraft if a wing can be made big enough to lift it. In fact, if you were in a building right now, it could probably fly if it had big enough wings stuck on it! Of course, there are other things needed like engines.

This force that lifts the aircraft is called lift. As the lift increases, the wing will bend. This is how it is designed. It can bend and it is meant to. In manufacture, they deliberately bend it with huge pulleys until they almost touch each other. It has to bend nearly all the way back before it does. Boeing used to have this on their website…

Anyway, during a flight it may bend up to twelve feet on a Boeing aircraft and this is normal and safe. It bends like a suspension system if that helps you think of it differently. If it did not bend, it would snap. So, a moving wing from here on is a good thing as you stare out of your window.

If it is still difficult to imagine that the movement of air can lift something heavy like a 747 or some of the newer huger aircraft arriving, then think of what air can do in some regions of the world. A tropical storm (air with attitude) that includes a hurricane can rip houses out the ground. These winds are often in the region of 100 mph. Air has power and commercial airlines know how to make the most of its positive elements.

Summary:

1. The wing is made big enough to lift the object it is attached to.

2. Air is strong and commercial airlines know how to make the most of it.

3. Pilots manage the lift and the other forces acting on an aircraft to maintain flight.

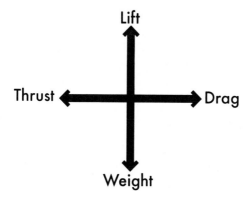

A simple diagram of what pilots manage

Imagine an aircraft sat right in the middle of the cross pointing towards the thrust arrow. This is what the pilots manage all the time to maintain flight. Incidentally, once the aircraft is up there it just wants to fly – it is doing what it was designed to do.

And, the more fuel used the lighter the aircraft becomes and therefore the more lift available!

The Tail

The tail of the aircraft is made up of two horizontal surfaces called the horizontal stabilisers and a vertical surface called the vertical stabiliser or fin. The vertical stabiliser is like a big shark fin but it is on top instead of underneath, like it would be on a ship. If you look closely at the big fin, you will notice that there are two parts. This is just a quick example of the extra capacity built into aircraft where there are back up systems for everything.

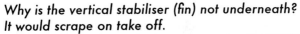

Why is the vertical stabiliser (fin) not underneath?
It would scrape on take off.

The horizontal stabilisers are small wings and produce lift in the same way as the main wing. They are much smaller than the main wing as they are only required to produce enough lift to balance the aircraft in flight.

The angle at which the horizontal stabiliser meets the oncoming air can be adjusted. This means that the balancing force can be changed as the aircraft weight and speed changes. The pilot does this manually when he / she is flying the aircraft, or it is done mechanically by the automatic pilot.

The vertical stabiliser gives the aircraft stability in YAW. This is the term used to describe side to side movement of the aircraft. It's completely normal and the same happens to ships.

In fact, the aircraft behave very similar to ships in water because the air has all the properties of water except that you can't see it.

Summary:

1. The tail has two parts to it and like all the other parts of the aircraft, there are back up systems.

2. It acts like a rudder on a boat, except it is only used for keeping the aircraft straight.

Control Surfaces

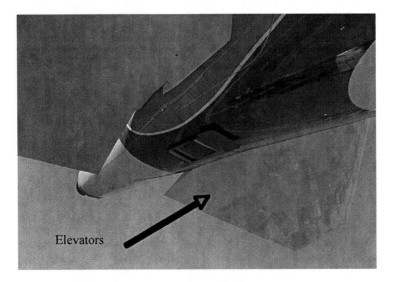

Elevators

Elevators are attached to the rear of the horizontal stabilisers. To put it simply, when they are moved up, the force produced causes the nose of the aircraft to rise, which enables the aircraft to climb. When they are moved down the force causes the nose of the aircraft to go down and this enables the aircraft to descend. This up or down direction is called PITCH.

Rudders are attached to the rear of the vertical stabiliser. They move left or right and just like the rudder on a boat, move the nose of the aircraft left and right. Unlike a boat, the aircraft is not turned by the use of rudders alone, but they help to balance the aircraft when in a turn.

Spoilers

Spoilers

Spoilers are attached to the surface of the wing. Their main job is to spoil the lift that is created over the wing (Remember the low pressure above the wing because Richard is travelling faster over the top?)

You will see a bank of spoilers come up when the aircraft has landed. This is because aircraft are so well designed for flying that the lift has to be spoiled once you are on the ground.

During a flight, you may see small spoilers coming up. This is to help the aircraft to turn or BANK, or to act as speed brakes to slow the aircraft down. This means the aircraft can turn extremely elegantly and is a bit like some modern trains that can tilt when they go around corners. You may not even notice onboard the aircraft as they never turn more than about 30 degrees angle or 'bank' which is not much.

Ailerons

These are found on the rear of the wing. There are four on each aircraft, two either side. They work in opposition to each other and are used to help aircraft bank.

If you are particularly excited at the prospect of being able to spot when the aircraft is banking, you need a flat table and a gin and tonic! Place the gin and tonic on the table and then watch it avidly for 10 hours. The gin and tonic will act like your own little spirit level and you will soon be the envy of your friends and family as you spookily point out accurately every time you bank!

Flaps and slats

Flaps and slats are fitted to the front and rear of the wing. These have been one of many great innovations over time as the aircraft have evolved. Early aircraft had fixed wings which could not change shape. This limited the speed, height and duration that the aircraft could fly for. Flaps and slats change the wing so that it can fly at both high and low speeds. They fold or slot neatly away when the aircraft is flying at faster speeds. When the aircraft needs to fly more slowly, as in take off and landing, the flaps (and slats) are brought out in stages to alter the shape and size of the wing. See next page:

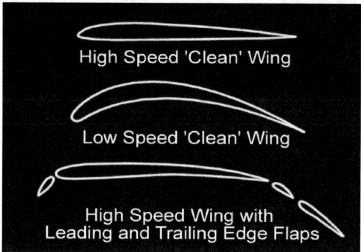

High Speed 'Clean' Wing

Low Speed 'Clean' Wing

High Speed Wing with
Leading and Trailing Edge Flaps

When you are looking out of the window(!) you will notice the amount of flap varies depending on the aircraft performance needed. The full amount of flap is only used for landing as this enables the aircraft to fly at its slowest speed.

By the way, when the flaps and slats come out, you WILL be able to see through the wing. This is normal and is not in any way a design fault or a sign of imminent doom!

Landing Gear

The landing gear, or undercarriage as it is sometimes known, differs in arrangement and design depending on the aircraft type. Generally, the bigger the aircraft, the more undercarriage legs and wheels there will be. The Boeing 747 has five legs and eighteen wheels. They are arranged in a way that enables the weight of the aircraft to be evenly distributed between the wheels.

Nose leg

The nose leg has two wheels. Each of the four main legs is situated under the centre of the aircraft where the fuselage is fitted to the wing. Each leg has four wheels. The aircraft is steered at slow speeds on the ground by moving the nose wheels to help the aircraft turn around sharp corners. Once the aircraft is moving fast down the runway, the rudder is used to keep it straight.

Once the aircraft is in the air, the landing gear is raised. Large doors open and the legs retract into the body and the wings. Just before landing, the doors open again and the landing gear is lowered and locked in the down position. You will notice this noise every single time you fly. It is a normal noise and can be quite loud as huge hydraulic systems are used to lift the wheels up. And, of course, there are back up systems for the wheel lifting hydraulics.

Each of the main wheels has large disc brakes. A very sophisticated breaking computer ensures that pressure is applied evenly so that the aircraft stops in a straight line. Initially, the brakes are applied automatically which enables them to be activated in the shortest time possible once the main wheels are on the runway. Once the aircraft has slowed down, the pilot controls the brakes using foot pedals that are attached to the rudder controls. As with all automatic systems, the pilot can override it if required.

Engines

Modern aircraft engines are very reliable. Many years ago, most aircraft were powered by piston engines working on the same principle as a car engine. Instead of driving wheels, they turned a propeller that pulled the aircraft through the air.

With the invention and development of the jet engine, reliability has improved beyond all recognition. Now twin-engine aircraft fly regularly across the North Atlantic which is something that would not have been possible, or allowed, many years ago.

An even more reliable type of jet engine called the High By-Pass Turbofan is now used to power modern commercial aircraft. It is a quieter and more efficient type of jet engine made up of three basic parts.

At the front is a large encased fan. This fan acts like a propeller and creates approximately seventy-five percent of the thrust. The air drawn in by the fan is passed out of the back of the engine without ever being mixed with fuel. This helps to quieten the engine noise by the way.

The rest of the air is compressed and mixed with fuel before it is ignited in a combustion chamber. This air then expands rapidly and after passing over turbines independently connected to the fan and compressor, passes out of the back of the engine producing the rest of the total thrust.

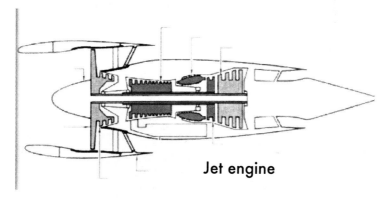

Jet engine

Engines are attached to the aircraft in different ways, the most common being on pylons below the wing. These pylons are designed to flex and move, so if you see this when you fly it is all perfectly normal!

Pylon

Jet Engines are big powerful things these days. Bird strikes are not a problem to these monsters. Flying cabin crew in your engine could be though...

All aircraft designed and certified to fly under the public transport category are capable of flying on less than the number of engines fitted. Engine failures and shutdowns are very rare. If it does happen, the pilots have already carried out many practices in a simulator and will follow safe and well planned procedures to bring the aircraft to a suitable airport for a normal landing.

Weather and Turbulence

Public transport aircraft are designed to fly in virtually
all weathers. Landing in fog is now commonplace. Many
aircraft carry out automatic landings in visibility down to
just 75 metres. If the visibility is less than this, or if the
aircraft is not equipped with auto land, it will divert to
another airport where the weather is better.

The atmosphere is constantly changing. Like the sea, which
is affected by the movement of warm and cold currents,
the cold and warm air masses moving over the Earth give
rise to vertical movement, which is all that turbulence
consists of. The more rapid the change in temperature, the
greater the movement of the air. The aircraft is able to ride
the bumps, moving up and down just a few feet at a time.
The air is a fluid and just as there are no holes in the sea,
there are also no holes in the air. Air pockets therefore do
not exist.

Turbulence is not a danger to aircraft but must be respected
by the passengers and crew and this is why we switch the

seat belt signs on in areas of turbulence. We also strongly recommend that you keep your seat belt fastened when seated so that if the aircraft did enter an area of unforeseen turbulence, you would be perfectly safe. This does not mean that it is not safe to walk about to stretch your legs or visit the toilets. A sensible compromise is called for.

Clear Air Turbulence.

Please see picture below of Clear Air Turbulence.

As you can see, you can't see Clear Air Turbulence! Clear air turbulence (CAT) can sometimes be forecast and 'ride reports' for aircraft are given over the radio so that seat belt signs can be switched on ahead of the turbulence. For the aircraft to descend or climb to a 'smoother' altitude, the pilot will try to negotiate with Air Traffic Control. This is not always possible, but if you are in your seat with the seat belt fastened, then you are always safe.

Thunderstorms are associated with the more severe forms of turbulence. All aircraft carry weather radar which is always on at night or when flying in cloud. These huge clouds show up well on the radar so pilots are able to avoid them. If there is one over your destination when the aircraft arrives, the flight crew will wait until it has passed before landing or will go to another airport where the weather is better.

If a thunderstorm is forecast, then the crew will have taken on extra fuel so that they can wait for it to clear. If a storm is over the airport when the aircraft is due to take off, the crew will delay until it has cleared. They always carry extra fuel. The airlines you fly will have enough to hold for 30 minutes minimum and still fly to another pre-decided airport if needed.

The Flight

We suggest that you arrange your travel to the airport so that you arrive in good time. Why not even stay the night before locally so that you remove the last minute stress. Airports are busy and can appear chaotic to the non-nervous. Why not give yourself the best chance of feeling relaxed by building in more time than you need. A lot of research is carried out by the Airport Authorities around the easiest way to help passengers navigate around the airport. Different size signs and different positions and heights for the signs are tried with different levels of successful reading by passengers. The reality is that once you get to the airport, you are in a foreign environment to you. Those working at the airport can become quite blasé about finding their way around. For you, the infrequent visitor, it can be quite daunting trying to find your way around. Short message – build in time to get lost!

You could consider even checking in online before hand as that will save you a lot of hassle when you get there.

Most airport terminals are now mini shopping malls so there's plenty to do when you get there.

As you enter the terminal (great name for an airport building isn't it?!) you will notice a number of television screens that will indicate the check in area or zone for the airline that you are flying with. If you go online, you are able to get a layout for most airports to help better prepare you for where you go to when you arrive.

Do tell the ground staff that you are a nervous flyer. In fact, even better, contact the airlines Special Assistance department before you fly. Most airlines have a department set up to help people with particular needs including fear of flying. Virgin's department has been in operation since they set up, tirelessly helping people like you. If you phone, they will let the cabin crew know that a nervous person is on board so that the cabin crew can help you should you need it. Their number at the time of writing is 0870 380 2004.

At the check-in desk your ticket and passport will be inspected. The agent will ask you questions about how many bags you have in addition to various other questions. Be prepared to be asked questions and even searched. This is all part of the process. It is normal and it may even feel a bit weird to you as you start to realise that as you are handed your boarding card, you are now part of a process. This is the best and safest way to deal with lots of people on a daily basis. It can feel a bit impersonal, but that is for your safety.

At the airport, the best thing that you can do is to keep everything handy like passports, tickets and money so that you know where everything is. Allow plenty of time for busy periods and for the walk to where your aircraft is being prepared for you. By the way, whilst you are queuing to be searched and your bags to be scanned, so are the crew that will be flying with you. They go through all the same checks every time they fly. It is a thought to hold that as you take off your shoes, belts, watches, jackets and money from your pockets before going through the scanners, the crew do this all the time. Security is important and is there for all of our benefit.

When you get through immigration and security, you can wander around sampling the many retail outlets and eat – if you have allowed yourself extra time. If you are not sure how long you need to allow for your flights, all of this can be found on the airport website that you are travelling from. Being prepared gives you control over what you can control. Your bags and belongings are now someone else's responsibility to get to the aircraft.

As you wander around the Duty Free Shops (we are not on commission to write this), the cabin crew and pilots are already onboard the aircraft doing their security checks and making sure all the safety equipment is on board. Once that is done, they check the food is there – that is the order all airlines work in. Safety first – Always!

Once you are called for your flight, there is plenty of time to walk to your flight and get onboard. There is no need to sprint to the gate to just wait around a bit more. Allow time and then you can take your time. It will not help for you to arrive sweaty and nervous.

Onboard, the doors are closed and the cabin crew will start talking to you on the PA as people are settling into their seats. The cabin lights may flash, call bells may ding and dong – all completely normal and not secret messages from the crew.

Some of the many pieces of equipment that the crew will be checking while you shop!

Taxi

Before you taxi to the runway, you may be aware of the aircraft reversing and then being pulled along before the engines are started. Once the engines are started, the aircraft will trundle in a controlled manner to the runway. Some airports, such as JFK in New York, you seem to taxi for ages until you get to the runway. This is normal.

You will hear various noises as the pilots are checking the flaps by extending them and the flying controls are checked. If you are near the window you will see the controls move and the wing get bigger as the flaps are extended. Yes, you will see concrete between the wing and the flaps – this is normal.

As the aircraft proceeds to the runway, the cabin crew will demonstrate the emergency procedures. This can be either done manually by the crew or will be a short film. This is a requirement by law to be listening so you will be asked to turn off MP3 players or equivalent.

Now, believe it or not, this is the time to keep practising your deep breathing and the cognitive techniques to bolster your coping mechanisms. You are not in control of the flight like you might think you are in control during driving for instance, but the people that are in control are brilliant at what they do. This is a highly regulated and extremely safe industry. You won't necessarily meet the pilot but know this. She or he have been through rigorous training and re-training and are tested time and time again for their competence. They have families too! You are now in good hands so sit back and relax. Flying is safe because nothing is left to chance.

Take off

Once clearance has been given by Air Traffic Control (ATC), the aircraft lines up on the runway.

You will hear a call bell which lets the cabin crew know it is time to take their seats for take off. The senior cabin crew member will have been in contact with the flight deck to inform the captain that the cabin is secure and ready for take off.

Once on the runway, the final checks will have been completed. To get to this point, the crew will have carried out many lists of checks from the time they arrived at the aircraft.

The engine power increases slightly as the flight deck crew check that all the engine indications are normal. The engine power then builds to required thrust for take off and the aircraft accelerates to take off speed. The total time on the runway depends on the weight of the aircraft, but will be in the region of 40-60 seconds until you are away.

Once the calculated take off speed is reached, the pilot will raise the nose to allow the aircraft to fly off the runway. The degree of climb will vary for different aircraft types and weights but about 15 degrees is the average.

In the unlikely event that the aircraft ever did have an engine failure at this point, it could still take off. This is because that is the calculation already worked out by the pilots long before they even got to the runway.

Under carriage retracting

The first main noise you will hear is the undercarriage doors opening, followed by the wheels retracting into the wings and fuselage. The doors then re-close to cover the undercarriage legs and wheels.

Depending on the aircraft, airport and noise procedures, the engine power will be reduced at around 1500 feet after take off. The nose of the aircraft will be lowered slightly, the engines will go a little quieter and their may be whirring noises. This is not a great change in pitch of the aircraft at all. However our primitive land dwelling sense organs in our ears will very briefly, falsely detect this as if we are descending and the engines have stopped working! This is a normal feeling and happens every single time you fly. The trick is to talk to yourself and recognise that whilst you feel like you are descending with no engines on, you are not. You are still climbing with the engines about three quarters of the noise you previously had. This procedure is regulated to stop people who live near airports having their lives disrupted every few minutes day and night!

Please remember that this is normal and happens every flight. Sometimes the flaps will come in before the engine noise decreases slightly or vice versa – all perfectly normal.

Climb and Cruise

Once all the flaps have been retracted, the aircraft will accelerate to its most efficient climbing speed and will be taken to its initial cruise altitude. This will vary with aircraft weight and other limits laid down by Air Traffic Control. As the aircraft's weight is reduced by the use of the fuel, so the altitude will be increased.

The next noise that you may hear could be the chime to indicate that you can, if you wish, unfasten your seatbelt and leave your seat. All airlines recommend that once you are back in your seat you re-fasten your seat belt. The cabin crew will then begin their duties.

As the aircraft reaches its cruise altitude, the engine power is reduced once again. Throughout the flight, you may hear the power increase again and the aircraft altitude change as the flight deck crew obtain clearance to change to another altitude. Depending on the type and length of flight, this may happen once or twice, or it may not happen at all.

Soon after the aircraft reaches its cruise altitude, an announcement may be made, usually by the pilot flying the aircraft, to give any information that is of relevance to the passengers. This may include the estimated arrival time at your destination, temperature outside and speed of travel. The destination time may vary and the crew will keep you informed if that happens. This is completely normal as Air Traffic Control strictly control all aircraft timings, altitudes and timings of all the aircraft to keep them all safely apart.

The cabin crew will perform the role that differentiates them from each airline which is the service (Remember safety is their first job always). Please remember that alcohol can have a greater effect in the air which will exacerbate your nervousness as you become more easily dehydrated. We strongly recommend that you drink lots of water on long flights.

Descent and Landing

Shortly before the flight deck crew begin the descent to the destination airport, another announcement will be made to update everyone on the latest estimated time of landing and what the weather and temperature are.

The engine noise will change as the power is reduced to allow the aircraft to descend. This will be accompanied by a slight change in the altitude as the nose of the aircraft is lowered. Sometimes air traffic control insist on a faster rate of descent that requires the use of the spoilers. These are the panels on the top of each wing. This gives a slight buffeting effect but again this is normal.

As the aircraft descends the cabin altitude is also reduced which can produce a feeling of slight pressure in your ears. Sucking a sweet, swallowing or yawning can help clear your ears. Cabin crew are very used to this so they can help if you need it.

Once on the approach to the runway, the undercarriage will be lowered and the final stages of flap extended. The undercarriage doors open first, followed by the wheels extending. The noise of the undercarriage doors closing will then be heard.

As the aircraft is slowed, the noise of the flaps as they are once again extended will occur form time to time. The engine noise will also vary as the aircraft is levelled or descended under the requirements of Air Traffic Control. The seat belt sign will be switched on ready for landing.

The noise of the engines change throughout the approach, until just before the aircraft touches down when the engine power is reduced to idle. Once the main wheels are on the runway, the brakes are applied, reverse thrust (very noisy engine wise) is selected and all the speed brakes will come up too (big flaps that stand up on top of the wing). Once again the engine noise will increase at this point, the nose wheel will touch and the aircraft will decelerate to taxi speed. As the aircraft taxis to the parking stand, the speed brakes and flaps are retracted.

Once the aircraft has stopped, the engines are shut down, the seat belt sign is extinguished and the doors are opened. You are then able to leave the aircraft for the start of your holiday or business trip.

The Go Around

This is another very normal procedure that may have caused some of you discomfort as you may not have known what is going on. If at any time during the approach to the runway, air traffic control or the flight crew decides that they are not able to land, the aircraft will undertake a go around.

This decision will be taken for many reasons. The most likely cause is that there is an aircraft that hasn't quite cleared the runway in time. There are still huge safety margins built in here and the last check is made by the pilots as they decide whether to land or not. Alternatively, in bad weather, the crew have to be completely happy with their visual references they see when they come out of the cloud. It may be safer to go around and make another approach when the weather has improved.

What you would feel is a sudden change in the aircraft's pitch and the noise of the engines as they increase in power. Once the aircraft is climbing, the procedure is the same as during the take off. The crew practice this in the simulator every six months or so, although rare to you it is completely safe and normal manoeuvre. As soon as the captain is less busy, he or she will make an announcement. This may be a few minutes after the Go Around as they are focusing on flying safely and comfortably for you. Once they are able to do so, they will talk to you – there is nothing to worry about.

Please remember, flying is safe. Nothing is left to chance. Every part of the journey that you are on has been thought about and there are back up systems and plans for everything. Safety comes first and it is the safest way to travel.

Cabin Crew Training

David Gott - Senior Cabin Safety Trainer

Cabin crew are here for your safety as their primary role. The service they provide onboard the aircraft is the difference between airlines. Safety is a constant and all airlines have to meet internationally agreed levels of training.

The initial training for cabin crew is made up of three parts:

- Service Training
- Aviation Medicine Training
- Cabin Safety Training

Service training is what you see. The Aviation Medicine and Safety Training you may not be aware of.

The standard for this training is an 88% pass mark. This is pretty consistent across all airlines. The Wings that crew wear are truly earned – even if you can get them on eBay now!

Aviation Medical Initial Training

- Headaches/nosebleeds
- Cardiac arrest
- Childbirth

There was a time that this was just called First Aid Training. But this has changed due to how much cabin crew have to know now about onboard treatment. cabin crew are trained to deal with anything from nose bleeds right through to delivering babies.

First Aid Kit

Some of the medical equipment we keep on board now. The first aid kits are where you will find plasters, aspirin etc. The De Fib is the equipment that could re-start your heart if it stopped. The Doctor's kit can only be used by a medically qualified person.

De Fib

Sometimes people are concerned about what will happen to them if they are ill onboard. There is no better place to be unwell as the crew are trained in so many medical areas now. They also have the 'phone a friend' option.

Doctors kit

Medlink are a company attached to an Emergency Department in Arizona with 16 on call Aviation Trained Doctors available. They have access to more than 45 medical specialities and can advise on diversion hospitals at the different airports if needed.

This sort of valuable information allows the pilots to make the right decisions about where to divert in order to give you the best care possible.

Cabin Safety Initial Training

- Flight Safety
- Equipment Locations and Usage
- Restraint
- Emergency Procedures
- Security

Final Exam and Wings!

Cabin crew are trained in everything that they need to know to ensure a safe and manageable flight every time they fly. This ranges from knowing instantly where all of the safety equipment is stowed and checking it before every flight to make sure it is serviceable. They are taught how to restrain unruly passengers should this become necessary and carry the equipment should we need to contain somebody that may be of danger to you and the safety of the aircraft. Unfortunately, most disruptive behaviour is normally alcohol related. Did you know that one drink in the air is roughly equivalent to two drinks on the ground?

All crew are fully trained in how to carry out any Emergency Procedures that could be necessary in relation to the aircraft.

Both flight crew and cabin crew have security training. It would not be appropriate to discuss the security training, suffice it to say, there is a lot more going on behind the scenes than you will ever hear about.

At some point whilst you are moving away from the terminal, you will hear an announcement saying something like 'Doors to Armed or Doors to Automatic and cross check.' The cabin crew move a small lever on the doors which mean it is then ready to be used as an emergency exit.

If we were needed to evacuate the aircraft, it becomes a huge slide as below.

If we were to open the door in water, instead of a slide, it becomes a raft. It is not like the Titanic, there are ample more spaces than are needed.

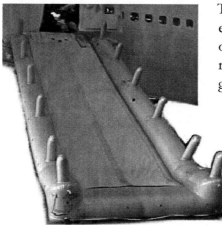

The slide rafts are equipped with all sorts of back up such as radios, flares, water and glucose sweets.

123

The Safety Demonstration

This is absolutely required by law and will happen each and every time that you fly. It can be done either manually or via video format. We really do urge you to listen to this as procedures can be slightly different for each airline and aircraft type.

It is not there to scare you.

Every time humans come together for a meeting of any sort in a public place, there has to be some form of safety briefing.

Safety demo by Lisa Condell

Lights and Chimes

Cabin crew use different Bings and Bongs to get their messages to each other. They are not secret messages. It is a long way to walk down a Boeing 747 just to ask if they have any of the chicken dinner left! The crew will always tell you if there is anything that you should know. Please always know that there is no conspiracy going on.

Special Assistance

Did you know that most airlines have some form of special assistance department that can help you? The Virgin number is here but most airlines can put you through from their reservations department. Do let your airline know that you are a nervous passenger so that they can help you more on board. There is also help available for wheel chairs users, the visually impaired and the deaf or hard of hearing.

(Virgin Atlantic) Telephone: **0870 380 2004**

Effective techniques to overcome your fear of flying

Notes from one of our seminars.

Fact.

You were not born with your fear. You have learned it or it has been triggered by something else.

This is great news. It means that you can learn to do something else. We can do three things together in these notes:

- Understand a little bit more about how the fear works in relation to your brain.

- Understand old patterns of fearful behaviour.

- Build some new healthier patterns.

"To have only one option is no option; to have two options is just a dilema; to have three options is a good start."
Charles Handy

Understanding your fear.

We have options open to us. Consider this question:

Is it possible, in theory, that you could live your life without this fear?

Answer: YES. It is possible in theory – anything is possible in theory.

Let us move into practically what is going on in your body in terms of fear and then take it from there to move into how we can break the patterns before building new ones.

Your Brain.

I am sure you would agree that having a brain is a pretty good thing. The trouble with having a brain is that there is a lot we don't know about how it works. Scientists are finding more and more amazing things that this sophisticated processing unit can do.

One of the things that we know is that the brain is performing millions of functions every second with absolutely no effort from us whatsoever – it is all automatic. It is super fast processor that has been fashioned over thousands of years of evolution. These notes will give you some clues how we can make the most of recent brain research.

Your brain learns very quickly. It is what Richard Bandler calls 'One trial learning' – it does not need to learn more than once something that is perceives as scary. It is there to protect us automatically. It has automatic responses built into the wiring when danger is sensed.

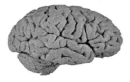

The complex brain is made up of million and millions of neurones

127

When we learn something, a connection is made in the brain. The brain looks around and finds similar experiences to link things into. Your brain has made some pretty strong connections around fear. For some of you, your fear is so great that just the mere mention of airports or seeing one on the telly is enough to trigger feelings of fear. The brain is that clever when it comes to protecting you – it immediately senses danger and then certain chemicals are activated to protect you. Just think of it, you can feel scared even when there is nothing around to be scared of – really useful.

As the connections become stronger, it is like having motorways that join up all the different memories together. All the feelings and chemicals that are activated become more easily activated but it does not have to be that way. You really do get more of what you pay attention to. The more you think about being scared, the better and quicker you get at it.

Later in this section and on our courses, we are encouraging people to create new pathways in their head when they think about aircraft. Instead of travelling down the fear highway, we are encouraging to take a different path. These different routes are a bit like dirt tracks at first because they are less travelled than the fear highways.

The Danger Radar

There is a small part of your brain that is constantly alert for danger. It is called the Amygdala. This small part of the brain, once alerted to any perceived danger, activates the fight or flight responses all animals possess. In humans, it means that as soon as you perceive danger, the thinking part of your brain starts to shut down as you respond in the more automatic way of fight, flight or freeze.

128

Danger radar

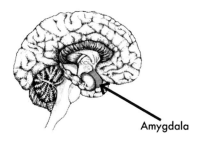

Amygdala

The Amygdala

- Always on duty.

- Extremely sensitive (Professor Daniel Goleman Research).

- Once activated, shuts down thinking.

- Once activated, rational thinking becomes harder to do.

- Main job to protect us

Have you noticed that once you start to feel fearful, you are less able to be 'talked out of it' by logical well meaning relatives or friends?

Things can be done about it and this will be covered in the section 'building new healthier patterns.'

Quick recap. **If** you have been practising getting scared and building super scared highway connections in your brain, what you perceive as danger will be entirely unique to you. As your Amygdala starts to sense what you perceive to be danger, your body will become flooded with get ready for action chemicals. This can start to shut down your thinking. **However**, according to Professor Goleman of Harvard University, this can be controlled as the first wave lasts for about 90 seconds.

Knowing that this is normal and would happen to every human that senses danger means that you can start to rationalise it. If you know that it is possible for this to happen to you when near an aircraft, you can plan what to do the moment it happens.

If you can stop the process after the 90 seconds by doing something else, you can regain control. If you don't plan what you will do if you feel this sort of anxiety signal occurring then you will be lost in the moment. You may also become more aware of what other people might think of you and so put yourself under more pressure.

In fact, it is fair to say that a lot of our clients are deeply concerned about making a fool of themselves. I am reminded of a quote from Eleanor Roosevelt, 'You would not worry what people thought of you if you realised how seldom they do.'

Fear is there to protect us

You were not born with this fear but you were born with fears. Beck believes that fear is there to protect us. It acts as a limiter when we are going to do something dangerous and can activate chemicals that give us motive power to get out of the current situation.

When our Amygdala senses possible danger, it starts to shut down the more thinking part of the brain as we said above. The other parts of the brain are activated and we are ready to deal with the perceived danger.

At this moment, there is a flood of Adrenaline in the body and the person reacts. The effect tends to get called various names such as Anxiety Attack, anxiety disorder and sometimes panic attacks.

If you suffer from anxiety attacks, you may have experienced any or all of the following symptoms:

- During: Heart beats faster, sudden onset of apprehension, terror, feel like going crazy, unreality, sweaty palms, narrowed vision, thoughts of doom and dying, feel like having a heart attack, run off, not able to listen, and others...

- Afterwards: Rationalisation, intellectual resistance, embarrassment, relief, removal, justification, sleep...

Whatever name you call it, clearly these symptoms would not be pleasant for the recipient at all.

There is some good news though.

The trigger for these symptoms starts when your Amygdala picks up a danger signal from the surroundings. If you have been practising being scared and this can be triggered by anything at all related to flying whatsoever, then the Amygdala will start to stimulate the chemicals needed for action (Via other parts of the brain but that is not relevant for now).

The first wave or feeling of anxiety starts. This, when backed up with automatic thoughts of doom and disaster, create insta-panic if we are not careful. At this moment, we have to STOP and do something different.

I will go so far as to say, that there is a lot that can be done beforehand to prepare ourselves well in advance of even coming near to our individual triggers. We will cover this in the third section on building new patterns.

Filling in the Gaps

As you look at the picture, you can clearly make out the shape of a cube. There is no cube there just white space. Our brain, when presented with incomplete information, fills in the gaps.

This book is about giving you the right information to fill in those gaps. So, next time you hear an odd noise and you don't know what it is, you can fill in the gaps with the right answers. Without the correct knowledge from us (rather than the well meaning, seemingly all-knowing relative that gives you facts he or she read in the newspaper!)

Old Patterns

When we wander around and talk to people at the beginning of our courses, we ask them what they are scared of. Below, in no particular order, is what people talk to us about in terms of their fear:

The ability to imagine their demise in intricate detail. The image that they find very easy to replay is their death in glorious Hollywood style Technicolor. There will be sound effects and they are quite clear exactly how they will die in their personal movie clip. One client told me once, 'I don't seem to be able to get over my fear of flying and every time I go near an airport, I can see myself plummeting towards the ground at 900 miles an hour!'

- *Catastrophizing.* As the brain fills in the gaps, imagining the worst. For example, two call bells going off in quick succession = Secret message between the crew. Cabin crew member frowning as he walks down the cabin aisle hurriedly = he is moving to the furthest point of impact – 'cos he knows something.

I wonder which one I shall be today...

- *Intellectual Resistance.* This is called Cognitive Dissonance by coaches and trainers like me. This means when a person's mind is so set on their current set of beliefs, it becomes hard to let in new ideas. For example, 'I don't care what you tell me! I know we hit an air pocket because I felt us plummet!' That is an extreme example but a simpler one can be when someone is absolutely convinced that they will always have this fear and nothing you can do will stop them having it.

- *Conditioned Responses.* This is where the person, without realising it, has set up some very powerful responses to flying. For example, the mere glimpse of an aircraft flying overhead triggers a lightening reaction of starting to hyperventilate. Conditioned responses occur because they are behaviours that have been re-enforced over time. If repeated enough, they become instant and don't even have to be thought about – we will look at breaking this link later.

- *Automatic Thoughts.* This is similar to a chatterbox in one's head. Thoughts are going on all the time in our heads whether we are aware of them or not. Cognitive Psychologists believe that thoughts precede feelings which are linked to chemicals. If we automatically are thinking, 'We are going to die, I am not safe' etc. we are creating chemicals in ourselves ready to react to the perceived danger.

- *Concept of Vulnerability.* This is the last concept which we notice sometimes. People can feel vulnerable about living regardless. This can manifest when we have our own children or our parents or carers start to get older. No-one quite knows why this fear of vulnerability attaches itself to the safest form of transport when we know logically; it is more dangerous walking next to a road or driving a car. One theory suggests that flying is a time when we are least in control of our environment and what happens to us. This has been extended to people who don't like hospitals too.

You're breathing too much!

Another fascinating area, to look into on the Internet if you are as interested as we are, is Breath research.

According to Professor Robert Freedman, we all average about 12-15 breaths per minute or maybe more. This is shallow breathing which tends to be from the top of the chest which means we are not getting enough oxygen into our blood. This is fascinating because when there is a lack of oxygen in our blood, it automatically activates our Sympathetic Nervous System. This is linked to guess what? Our flight or fight instinct!

In other words, if we are breathing incorrectly most of the time, we are already in a state of mild anxiety on a daily basis. Feeling calm is a bit like a bucket with a small hole in it. Life throws stuff at us all the time to keep us from breathing correctly and feeling calm. For example, being late for work, getting stuck in traffic, arguing with your family... All of these things take their toll. Out of the hole go your feelings of calm. The bucket has to be topped up or you may just collapse. What do you do to re-fill the ever emptying bucket?

Add in the fear of flying, and you are already a couple of notches along the fearometer.

How relaxed are you? Answer yes or no. Look at the number of times that you say yes or no.

Quick Quiz...

Question	Yes or No
Are you able to relax without feeling guilty?	
Do you find it easy to unwind?	
During the day, can you turn off and just let go of pressures?	
Do you have a plan for relaxing on a daily basis?	
Are you able to stay under control when you feel under stress?	
Total	

Take a moment to reflect on your answers. What could you do to keep your general levels of calm at a better level?

Over-breathing equals panic attacks?

If you are breathing faster than you need to, you are more likely to stimulate your sympathetic nervous system. This is most closely linked to your flight or fight response. In other words, if you are already slightly over-breathing, you are nearer to someone hyperventilating than somebody who is breathing at the recommended 6-8 breaths per minute.

As I mentioned earlier, this over-breathing is stimulating the fight or flight response. This could make you panic more until you have an anxiety attack which we looked at above.

Anxiety Attacks – The Facts

- Panic attack peaks in 10 minutes.

- You can't die from one (NHS Direct).

- People often go to hospital emergancy rooms many times before being correctly diagnosed. (Raymond Richmond PHd).

- Having one does not make it more likely to repeat.

- Paradoxically, fearing another attack might happen unwittingly brings it on (Beck and Coue).

So, you can't die from a panic or anxiety attack. No-one knows why some people's level of fear goes to an anxiety attack and why some people do not. From the National Institute of Mental Health, 'Heredity, other biological factors, stressful life events and thinking in a way that exaggerates bodily reactions are believed to play a major role in the onset of panic disorder. No-one knows the exact cause though.'

So, we don't know for certain why people get them. We do know we can't die from one. We also know that what we think can help us not to 'exaggerate bodily reactions.' In other words, part of the help in the 'Building New Patterns' section is to change the automatic body reactions/ programming that we have set up. We will also introduce you to Counter Conditioning which is something that you can do now, in preparation for your flight and especially when queuing at various different locations in airports. With the increased security at Airports now, you need to prepare to wait and have a strategy to keep your brain occupied.

Building New Patterns

What can be done?
Breaking the old patterns

1. Neuro Linguistic Programming

2. Cognitive Behaviour Therapy

3. Breath Research

What I am going to introduce is a mixture of these three approaches above. This, combined with the knowledge that you have gained from our questions being answered plus the technical knowledge, will put you on the right track.

We use a mixture of these three on our courses. We also use Desensitisation techniques. Within these notes you will also be able to use a form of Gradual Desensitisation that you can do anywhere and anytime.

So much jargon…

Name	Quick Description
NLP	Neuro Linguistic Programming. A curiosity about how some humans are able to do amazing things whilst others look on in awe. A range of techniques that help you to start doing things that you want to do and to stop doing things that you want to stop. Very simple.
CBT	Cognitive Behaviour Therapy. The belief that every behaviour we exhibit has some thought structure behind it. Listen to your thoughts, change them and the behaviour will change. Not everyone deals with the same situation the same way because their thinking is different.
Breath Work	Breathing properly to better stimulate our Parasympathetic nervous system which is sometimes called our relaxation response. Breathing properly means stimulating the diaphragm and breathing about 6-8 breaths per minute.
Rapid Desensitisation	Exposing somebody to their fear quickly so that they face the fear.
Gradual Desensitisation	Exposing somebody to their fear in a controlled manner. The combination of CBT and breath work helps here because you are able to face elements of your fear in a controlled manner. You process that particular part then move on.

Counter Conditioning	This is another name for Gradual Desensitisation. To change the conditioned pattern of seeing an aircraft with the onset of panic you need to change the response. In other words, if you always become fearful whenever you see an aircraft it becomes a conditioned response. If you gradually get used to seeing aircraft whilst in a relaxed state, then the automatic or conditioned or learned response changes to being relaxed instead of panicking.

Let's get started...

Exercise one: Fear Signals

1. List all of the stages of a flight. Starting with booking the ticket right through to arriving at the hotel the first day of the hotel. List all of the stages completely separately sparing no detail. Write the list and fully as possible.

   For example:

   1. *Phoning the travel agent*
   2. *Packing for the holiday*
   3. *Ordering a taxi*
   4. *Arriving at the airport*
   5. *Finding check-in desk*
   6. *Speaking to the airline staff*

2. Now, next to each item, write a score from 1-100 of how much that part of the journey bothers you. So each item should generate a score.

1. *Phoning the travel agent* 0
2. *Packing for the holiday* 40
3. *Ordering a taxi* 10
4. *Arriving at the airport* 85
5. *Finding check-in desk* 80
6. *Speaking to the airline staff* 60

3. This now gives you a pecking order for the different stages of your fear. These we will use in a moment after we have looked at breathing.

4. Next, we are going to discuss breathing again. Earlier, I said that you should be breathing less but fuller breaths. This is because diaphragmatic breathing is more likely to stimulate the parasympathetic nervous system – our relaxation response.

This is how you do it.

- Stand up

- Put hand in front of tummy.

- Breathe in slowly until tummy goes out.

- Breathe out slowly (tummy goes in).

- Diaphram breathing stimulates parasympathetic nervous system – relaxation response

This type of breathing is what I want you to combine with the earlier work we did on your 1-100 fear signals.

5. What we are going to do now is to practice gradual desensitisation. This will give you practical things that you can do between now and your flight. Gradual desensitisation has been found to be extremely effective. This is because you combine your 'fear signals' with relaxation. This is sometimes called counter conditioning. This works because we are going to reverse the automatic conditioning that you have already.

   i.   Old Response: Sight of airport = Panic

   ii. New Response: Sight of airport will be visualised whilst relaxed. This changes the automatic response gradually over time until it has less of a hold. (On our Flying Without Fear Courses we use other techniques but these don't translate into print so well – they are better done with us)

6. This technique is a bit like the equivalent of watching the same scary movie 20 times. The first time you will not know what to expect and your body will be flooded with adrenaline and other chemicals to get your body ready to react. Each time you watch the film, you would become more and more desensitized to the fear parts of the film until, eventually, you might even find them funny! Familiarity with the fear signals reduces their power as we are breaking the automatic conditioning that has been in place to date. In other words, familiarity breeds content; you will be content where you were not before.

Bringing it all together

1. Take three deep breaths using the type of breathing that I have mentioned above where your stomach goes in and out when you breathe. You can also practice using a relaxation CD.

2. When you feel relaxed, I want you to think of one of your fear signals that you listed earlier on. As you visualise fully your fear signal, I want you to breathe deeply. This is the Counter Conditioning technique where things that previously bothered you, now will cease to have the same hold over you – Familiarity breeds content.

3. In one session you can practice with up to three of your fear signals.

4. This is the technique that has been proven, over time, to reduce your fear of anything actually.

Research has found that it did not matter how the fear arrived at all. If it was a sudden onset or gradual over time, it made no difference to the speed of getting rid of the fear.

Sometimes fear of flying can be mixed up with lots of fears so it is better to isolate each part and deal with them separately.

Why not try this right now!

How did you get on?

This practising breathing whilst thinking about what you are fearful of has been shown to be extremely effective in beating your fears. The more you do it, the more that you can get to 'familiarity breeds content.'

Other Relaxation Exercises you can try...

This is another exercise that people have found extremely useful.

1. Once you are relaxed taking three deep breaths, imagine you are sat in the front room of your house / apartment.

2. The TV is going to come on in a moment and you are going to see a picture of your fears playing out in front of you. You are watching yourself in the image of the TV.

3. Next thing is to mess around with the image so that it loses its power. First thing you can do is to change the image from colour to black and white. If there is sound, turn it down. If it is a moving image, run the whole thing backwards at high speed. Do this messing around many many times. This breaks the pattern that the normal memory ran as. You are literally re-programming yourself.

4. Now put a new image on the screen with you dealing with your fear literally effortlessly. Imagine that you are there and everything is going great. You look relaxed and you are smiling. You are dealing with the thing that you used to be scared of with ease. You are at your best dealing with your fear as if you never had it.

5. Now for the interesting bit, imagine yourself stepping into the TV and becoming the person that is effortlessly dealing with your fear.

6. You can do this whole thing as many times as you like. You might be surprised to find that the whole fear element becomes less and less each time you practice.

While you Wait

It is a good idea to have some strategies to use while you wait around at the airport.

- Count and let go automatic thoughts.

- Spinning wheel.

- Paired Technique (Proper Breathing).

- STOP!

- Positive Affirmations (What ever happens is normal and I can cope).

Strategy 1 – counting automatic thoughts.

If we can accept that we do have these automatic thoughts in our heads. Thoughts of 'oh my God, I can't go through with this!' or, 'I am feeling uncomfortable now.' Just acknowledge them and count them as you wave them goodbye.

Strategy 2 – Spinning Wheel

Imagine that your fear is spinning in your stomach. Notice which way it spins. Next imagine the spinning fear coming out of your body and then imagine watching it spin in front of you. Now change the direction it spins to the other way. Put it back inside your tummy. Keep doing this until the fear decreases from 10 out of 10 to something you feel comfortable with.

Strategy 3 - Proper Breathing

Practice deep breathing (Tummy in and tummy out) – it is hard to be scared when you are breathing properly. When you feel scared, your breathing becomes shallow. Change your breathing = change your feelings/thoughts.

Strategy 4 - STOP!

Every time that you think of some image of death and destruction, imagine a huge STOP sign in your head and tell the image to go away. You get more of what you pay attention to. Keep practising seeing death images and you will get more of them!

Strategy 5 - Positive Affirmations

You really cannot afford the luxury of a negative thought. Keep positive statements in your head to drown out the negativity. 'I can do this.' 'Turbulence is uncomfortable but not dangerous.' 'I am a capable person.' 'Whatever happens is normal and I can cope with it.'

(By the way, if you don't believe this, try it before your next job interview – 'I am rubbish and will be rubbish in the interview and then see how you get on!)

Back to the brain...

IF you have been practising getting scared and building super scared highway connections in your brain, what you perceive as danger will be entirely unique to you. As your Amygdala starts to sense what you perceive to be danger, your body will become flooded with get ready for action chemicals. This can start to shut down your thinking. BUT, according to Professor Goleman of Harvard University, this can be controlled as the first wave lasts for about 90 seconds.

Knowing that this is normal and would happen to every human that senses danger means that you can start to rationalise it. If you know that it is possible for this to happen to you when near an aircraft, you can plan what to do the moment it happens.

As we said earlier, if you can stop the process after the 90 seconds by doing something else, you can regain control. If you don't plan what you will do if you feel this sort of anxiety signal occurring then you will be lost in the moment. You may also become more aware of what other people might think of you and so put yourself under more pressure.

Some easy strategies you can try:

- Practice some of the breathing techniques we have covered .

- Have a well practiced affirmation that you use at that moment. For instance, 'I am feeling anxious and that is okay. I am going to be okay. I am not in any danger. When I am ready, I will carry on.'

- Walk away from the trigger situation and get your thoughts together, drink some water and then give yourself permission not to be perfect and go back when you are calm again.

Final Words

We have really enjoyed writing this book. Our whole programme of courses and everything else that we do is borne out of a huge passion to help people to fly again or indeed for the first time.

All of the notes have been carefully written with you in mind.

If you want to know more about us please visit

www.flyingwithoutfear.info

Resources

Books:

Feel the Fear and do it anyway. Susan Jeffers

Awaken the Giant Within. Anthony Robbins

Using your brain for a change. Richard Bandler

Staying safe. Paul Christien

You cannot afford the luxury of a negative thought. John Roger & Peter McWilliams

REBT explained. Michael Neenan.

Websites:

www.airfraid.com

Courses:

Virgin Atlantic Flying Without Fear programme.

www.flyingwithoutfear.info

147

Glossary

Aerofoil
Attachment to aircraft whose shape is designed to produce the force of lift as air passes over it.

Lift
Force produced as air passes over an aerofoil to oppose the force of weight (gravity).

Stabiliser
A horizontal aerofoil at the back of an aircraft to stop the aircraft moving in pitch unless demanded by the pilot. Works with the fin like the flights on a dart.

Yaw
Movement of the aircraft about the vertical axis – i.e. moving the nose from side to side

Elevator
A control surface hinged on the back of the stabiliser. As the pilot moves it up or down, lift is decreased or increased on the stabiliser, causing the nose to move up or down

Pitch
Movement of the aircraft about the horizontal axis – i.e. moving the nose up and down

Aileron
A control surface hinged on the back of the wing near the wingtip. There is one on each wing and they move in opposite directions to each other. They are used by the pilot to roll the aircraft and make it bank.

Bank
Movement of the aircraft about the longitudinal axis – i.e. rocking of the wings

Flap
A control surface on the back of the wing that can be extended backwards to increase the surface area of the wing, and deflected downwards to increase the curvature of the wing. The flaps on both wings move together and are used to increase lift at lower speeds.

Spoiler

A control surface that can be extended from the top of the wing that both reduces lift and increases drag. Spoilers on both wings move together.

Drag

An aerodynamic force that tries to slow down the aircraft and dramatically increases as speed increases, or as flaps or wheels etc are lowered into the airflow.

CAT

Clear Air Turbulence – turbulence not associated with clouds, and often occurs where air moving at different speeds or directions meet. Usually easy to forecast.

Go Around

An aborted approach to land. The aircraft climbs back into the sky and flies around to approach the same runway again, or diverts to another airport.

Fin

A vertical aerofoil at the back of an aircraft to stop the aircraft moving in YAW unless demanded by the pilot. Works with the stabiliser.

High by-pass turbofan

A powerful, modern and quiet jet engine. Most of the air that passes through the large thrust producing fan at the front of the engine goes around the outside of the rest of the engine and bypasses the burners, fuel and turbines. The principle is that the engine pushes back a large amount of cool air slowly, rather than a small amount of hot air very fast. This is both quieter and more fuel efficient.

Rudder

A control surface hinged on the back of the fin. As the pilot moves it left or right an aerodynamic force is produced sideways on the fin, causing the nose to move left or right.

Index